The Old Homeplace

A Collection of Facebook Devotionals and Memories

John H. Voss

Parson's Porch Books

The Old Homeplace: A Collection of Facebook Devotionals and Memories
ISBN: Softcover 978-1-960326-45-4
Copyright © 2023 by John H. Voss

Parson's Porch Books is an imprint of Parson's Porch *&* Company (PP*&*C) in Cleveland, Tennessee. PP*&*C is a self-funded charity which earns money by publishing books of noted authors, representing all genres. Its face and voice is **David Russell Tullock** who you can contact at: dtullock@parsonsporch.com.

Parson's Porch *&* Company *turns books into bread & milk* by sharing its profits with the poor.

www.parsonsporch.com

The Old Homeplace

Contents

Preface

I have shared numerous devotionals on Facebook over the last five years. Most were biblically based, and others were reflections on life or humorous stories from my youth. Many of those were published earlier in "The Rainbow Book: A Collection of Facebook Devotionals." This book is a companion work.

This house and barn were built about 1925, and my grandparents moved here in 1932. Following their deaths, my uncle and aunt lived here many years, and the house became the center of Voss family life. The old homeplace became my residence in 2017, and I cherish the opportunity to call it home.

I am grateful to the many readers who have enjoyed these devotionals over the years and have commented on them. They have been a vital part of my writing work and interest. I am also especially grateful to Jeffery McClendon for his tireless work and meaningful contributions as an editor.

Many of my earliest memories are associated with the house and barn. I was able to take pictures of both that seem to capture the essence of "the old homeplace" that is dear to so many relatives and friends. I hope you enjoy the pictures, and I also hope that the devotionals are a great blessing to you.

Grandma's Dinner Bell

The old dinner bell has been in a storage shed here for years. Today, it got hung again. It wasn't easy because it's very heavy, but it now has a new life. It has a wonderful high-pitched ping when rung. I have no idea how old it is, but I can just imagine it being rung years ago to summon family members from the field chopping cotton to eat dinner. "Yall wipe your feet and wash your face and hands in the wash basin on the back porch. Somebody will need to draw a bucket of water from the well, but let the bucket down slowly or you'll muddy the water. There's a flour-sack towel hanging there and a bar of lye soap all of you can use. The biscuits will be ready in about three shakes of a sheep's tail. Don't get in a rush. Just hold your tater till the gravy cools."

As a little bare-footed boy, I often drew water from the well that still stands outside the backdoor. Oh, the memories and thoughts that one old dinner bell can ring out.

The Good Earth

In addition to the fragrance of flowers, two other things titillate my olfactory nerve and tell me it's springtime—freshly mowed grass and newly plowed soil. The sight and smell of good dirt will make any farmer or gardener want to put seed in the ground.

Most people don't appreciate the tenuous nature of topsoil in South Mississippi. In general, it's less than a foot deep and then one finds red clay, which isn't worth a hill of beans for growing anything but trees and Bermuda grass. Topsoil is highly erodible, and once it washes away, the process of restoring soil takes a very long time, if it can be done at all.

About a century ago, America had an enormous problem with eroding topsoil caused largely by poor farming practices. Through President Roosevelt's leadership, Congress enacted laws that created the Soil Conservation Service, and the construction of "terrace rows" and the practice of terraced farming brought great change to South Mississippi cotton and corn fields.

These elongated, raised earthen mounds controlled rainwater run-off and forced the water into roadside ditches rather than running downhill and eroding priceless topsoil. Terrace rows across pastures and fields still exist today.

Once the law was passed, then came the hard part. How were these long rows of elevated soil, stretching for hundreds of feet across a field, to be constructed? In those days, there were few large earth-moving machines available to an impoverished farmer, and so the work was usually done in a sweat-popping, back-breaking difficult method that no one would attempt today. They were built by hand with mules pulling a heavy metal "slip" that cut into the ground and filled with dirt. At the proper spot, the slip was flipped up and forward, dumping out the dirt, and the process was then repeated hundreds of times.

A slip full of dirt was very heavy and really needed two men lifting each long handle to flip it forward. If one man did it all day, you did not want to cross him because he was one strong rascal and could give you a whooping with one hand tied behind his back.

It's difficult for me to imagine, but my mother helped Grandpa Voss lay off the terrace rows on this old farm, and it was done in a very elementary manner. He set up a carpenter's saw horse on level ground, and then my mother put a carpenter's level on top of the saw horse and, while sitting on the ground, looked across the top of the level and sighted in grandpa as he moved along driving stakes in the ground on a level contour. It took hours and hours of work to lay off the terraces and then days and weeks of unbelievably hard work with mules and a slip to build the terrace rows.

All of this was done to then plant cotton that the boll weevils and Bermuda grass attacked. I don't know how they did it, but they did.

I love good dirt because it's a life-sustaining gift from God. I love to plant seeds in it, marvel at the growth of plants, and rejoice with thanksgiving at the bounty of fruits, flowers, vegetables, and other food that it produces.

Dirt is not dirty—it is priceless. On some warm spring day, hold a handful and marvel at its potential. Gaze at it for several moments, sift it through your fingers, smell it, and realize that it is the key to all the beauty and bounty of nature that you see around you. By all means, cherish it and preserve and protect it.

Say a prayer and thank God for the good life that the good earth provides you, and then thank Him for the strength and determination that He gave to our ancestors who worked incredibly hard to prevent this good earth from washing away.

The Fly Sprayer

It's importance cannot be over-stated, both from personal home comfort and social significance. The basic fly sprayer was indispensable and most every country home had one. Early on, many houses didn't have window screens, and flies from the barnyard and chicken house were a constant torment. But screened windows helped with that problem, with one exception—the back door. It was a fly magnet, and someone yelling from the kitchen, "Don't hold that screen door open, you'll let the flies in" is clear in my memory.

The answer was Watkins Fly Spray and the dependable old fly sprayer. The "Watkins Man" had the spray in the back of his old station wagon, along with an assortment of home necessities. I can still remember the fragrant smell when he opened the big, back door of that dusty, brown car.

The fly sprayer was used every day, and for good reason. There was no running water and dish water was heated on the stove and put in two large dish pans. The used dish water was then either thrown in the yard off the back porch or poured into "slop bucket" cans on the porch. That was taken to the barn and fed, along with some corn, to the hogs. Flies loved the slop buckets. To combat their swarming around the back door, a handful of cotton was wrapped in a string and tied to the middle of the screen door and then soaked with Watkins Fly Spray. That helped, but the hateful boogers still found their way inside.

That's where the social importance of the fly sprayer came into play. One of the big moments for any family was having the preacher come eat Sunday dinner. Usually two chickens were fried, because he could eat most of one by himself, and heaven forbid if a fly got in his gravy.

Let me share a personal example: Several years ago, I preached a Sunday sermon at a small country church and then went home with a wonderful family for dinner. It was Southern cuisine at its best—fried chicken, fried okra, fried squash. She may have fried the tablecloth for all I know because it was all stiff and starched. I did notice a couple of large chicken houses when I drove up, and I knew what that meant—flies. As we sat down to eat, one landed right in the middle of her coconut cake. No problem…just scoop it off with a spoon and keep going.

But just before taking my first sip of sweet iced tea, I noticed a big, black varmint floating in my tea. I quietly took the glass over to the lady where she stood at her sink, and I softly said, "I wouldn't hurt your feelings for anything, but there's something floating in my tea glass." She looked at it and exclaimed, "Well, what in tarnation is that?" She took the glass, and with a quick flick of her wrist and hand, sloshed the critter out, refilled my tea, and handed it back to me. Without missing a beat, she then smiled and asked, "You want biscuits or cornbread?" I totally enjoyed the meal, but I didn't drink much tea.

Just remember: If company is coming for Sunday dinner, especially the preacher, use the fly sprayer before they get there.

Do You Believe This?

I first encountered the reality of death on a Sunday afternoon in May 1954, three weeks after my sixth birthday. Grandpa Voss had been sick with throat cancer (probably from all those plugs of Brown's Mule chewing tobacco), and family members said he wouldn't last much longer, but death was a vague idea in my six-year-old mind. I had seen a few animals die, but not a human, and definitely not someone I loved.

The old house was filled with family and friends that day, and it seemed strange to me that no one laughed or smiled and some were crying. When I peeked into the front bedroom, grandpa was sleeping on his bed with family members forlornly looking down at him, and I didn't understand why. Usually they were laughing and talking, or eating the food neighbors had brought over, but not today. There was a strange atmosphere of quietness that filled the house, especially his bedroom, and everyone talked in a whisper. I had never seen anything like that.

At about 2:00 p.m., a couple of cousins and I were playing in the back of a 1952 Chevrolet pickup, parked in the cool shade of an old pecan tree, when an older cousin came out of the house crying and told us that Grandpa Voss was dead. I don't remember crying; in fact, I don't remember feeling much of anything except this strange and curious feeling about what death really meant.

I heard someone say that grandpa had gone to heaven to be with the Lord, but where was heaven and how did he get there? I knew he would never talk to me again and tease me, and I knew I probably couldn't sit by the wood-box beside the fireplace and build little houses with his plugs of chewing tobacco, while he rocked and spit tobacco juice into the fireplace, but to hear people talk about burying my grandpa in Coaltown Cemetery kind of scared me. He was my buddy, and I didn't want that done to him.

After a while, a doctor came and put one end of this rubber hose thing into his ear and the other end on grandpa's chest. He listened for a minute, and then said my dear old grandpa was indeed dead. He pushed his eyelids closed and pulled the bedsheet up over his face. There was no telephone in the house, so I guess someone went into town and called Colonial Funeral Home in Columbia, and they came and carried Grandpa Voss out of my life. I didn't really understand people's actions, because after they cried a few minutes, several went back to eating and laughing, and a lot of the men went outside and lit up a Prince Albert and talked about their stand of cotton that spring. Fried chicken and potato salad can be a soothing salve to a hurting Southern soul.

That was sixty-nine years ago, and the memory is still clearly etched in my mind. In the intervening years, I have watched several people die, both as a minister and also while working in hospitals. Most all of my older family members are now deceased, several people with whom I worked, my best friend of over fifty years, and I, too, have faced the reality of my own death through progressive heart disease.

I don't want to sound ghoulish, but the idea of death strangely fascinates me, and here's why: If you are a Christian, it doesn't exist! That sounds crazy, I know, but it's true. Jesus willingly entered into two things that are opposite to Him—sin and death—and destroyed their claim on our Christian life. We are no longer in bondage to either.

Jesus' great gift to us is eternal life. Because of His covenant with us, His life eternally becomes our life. That means we will live in heaven for as long as Jesus does! Jesus made some startling claims about death. Through His resurrection, He proved that death has lost its hold on us, but He also said, "I am the resurrection and the life. He who believes in Me, though he may die, he shall live. And whoever lives and believes in Me shall never die. Do you believe this?"

What an amazing promise! That literally means, in the words of scripture, that no grave can ever claim victory over me and that the sting of death has been rendered painless. It is no longer to be feared—it is forever meaningless, harmless, and of no effect in a Christian's life. I have pondered this passage hundreds of times, and I still can't truly fathom the enormity of Jesus' promise. Quite frankly, it is the most amazing and challenging statement in human history, in my opinion. But you must decide for yourself if you believe Him.

If what Jesus said is true, and I believe with all my heart it is, then Grandpa Voss isn't dead. None of my family and friends who placed their faith in Jesus as their Lord are dead. They are more alive than I am! They are painless, perfect, and pure in His holy presence, and in the glory of His heavenly kingdom, for all the ages to come.

One day, I shall join them. Because of the crucifixion and resurrection of Jesus, and because of my faith in Him as my Lord, the eternal consequences of sin and death are destroyed and are no longer a part of my human experience. My heart will stop one day and my eyes will close, but I won't be dead. Instead, that will be my passage to life everlasting.

That is Jesus' promise to you also, if you truly believe Him. I have been preaching and teaching the gospel of Jesus for over fifty years, and I have never understood why anyone would not respond to His redeeming love and to His promise of everlasting life. He will not force you; rather, He lovingly invites you to enter into the joy and fulfillment of His promises.

The question you need to answer this day is this: Do you believe Him?

The Bond of Generational Love

Memories of a Funeral

Time. Births. Deaths. Lives. Generations. The impact of time is most often viewed, I suspect, in the events of the present moment...the here and now events of each day. Yet time's greatest influence on our life extends across years, decades, and generations. Our family privately gathered last Sunday to remember the life of Barbara Voss and to inter her mortal remains. She was seventy-seven.

As a couple of family members assisted the funeral director in closing her grave, Barbara's great-grandson, William, helped. He is two—will be three in December. Interestingly, William was surrounded by generations of relatives about whom he knew nothing. He's too young to know, but their influence is stamped on his life. As he did his little part, in front of his great grandmother's grave is the grave of his great-great grandmother, Evelyn Voss, and to her side is the grave of William's great-great-great grandmother, Anna Taylor. She was born in 1885, Evelyn Voss was born in 1918, and William was born in 2020. That's a long span of time, but they helped prepare the way for the life this young boy will live as he matures into manhood.

William will not remember Grandmother Barbara. He's really too young to even understand who she was to him, and you might say he didn't really know her. But she knew him, and he knew and felt the warmth of her hugs, the comfort of being held in her arms, the sound of her laughter, and the tenderness of her touch.

William may have helped bury Grandmother Barbara's remains, but her love is buried in him and that can never be covered over and buried by age, disease, or disaster. She is forever a part of him, just as are Grandmothers Evelyn and Anna, and he is forever a reflection of them. Young William had no idea he was surrounded by one hundred thirty-eight years of love and family influence that will help shape William E. Gray into a fine young man. You can't bury that on a hot Sunday afternoon in July.

The Bible speaks of God visiting the negative influence of fathers upon their children to the third and fourth generations. Conversely, it stands to reason that God likewise extends the goodness of mothers and fathers to their children, grandchildren, and great-grandchildren to the third and fourth generations, and many more generations after that. The life and influence of Grandmother Evelyn and Grandmother Anna continue to live well beyond the grave in a child neither of them knew.

You can't bury generational goodness nor can you cover over a great-grandmother's love for a little blond-headed boy. William may not clearly remember what he did on that Sunday afternoon, but one day he will surely better understand the meaning of family love, and that bond of love and faith in God, stretching across generations, will help shape him into the man that God desires him to be.

Seven Generations

Alexander Voss. Who was he and what was he like? He lived many years before me, but I'm here due to him. He was the first in my family's line to immigrate to America from Germany, so he must have been courageous, daring, determined, and physically strong to endure the rigors of starting a new life in a new land.

He came to America about 1790 and married Mary Nichols. He became the father of Thomas Jefferson Voss, who fathered Charles Alford Voss. By that time, the family had migrated to the Sand Mountain area of north Alabama. Charles Alford fought extensively in the Civil War, and then married Martha Roe and became the father of James Holmes Voss.

James married Ella Carr and brought John Milford Voss into the world. Milford was my grandfather. He married Flora Sims and moved from Sand Mountain to Lumberton, Mississippi, and eventually to Purvis. His oldest son, John Milford Voss, Jr., married Evelyn Taylor. On April 13, 1948, their third son came screaming into the world. And I'm still here, going strong after seventy-five years and living in the same house grandpa and grandma moved into in 1932.

Six generations of German ancestry shaped by the bond of ancestral love and the blessings of America. Even though Voss is a rather common name in Germany (there's even a well-known street in Berlin named "Voss Strasse"), only a handful of us live in Lamar County.

Interestingly, my cousin and nephew both have Alexander for their middle name without knowing the family history. I've often wondered if Grandpa Alexander Voss could look down and see what his courage produced, would he smile and say, "Das ist gut!"

But I'm blessed with a bond of ancestral love that is even greater. The Voss family line may be my physical lineage, but I'm actually adopted. No, no, it's not some legal adoption that you may be wondering about. Let me explain what happened.

When I was ten years old, I became a believer in Jesus as my Lord and Savior. When I gave Him my life in faith, His Heavenly Father adopted me as a spiritual son. It's amazing, but that's what the Bible says happened. Jesus became not just my Lord, but He also became my spiritual brother. That's why He is referred to as the "first-born of many brethren." I became a joint-heir with Him to all the family love and blessings of our Heavenly Father.

This generational bond of divine love is so broad it's hard to describe. Since God adopted all who believe in Jesus the same way He adopted me, then all Christians are my brothers and sisters, and we are bound together as one big family of God with a bond of generational love that can never be broken or diminished.

My goodness, if you're reading this and you are a believer in Jesus too, then I'm writing this to my brothers and sisters! We may have never met, but there is a bond of love between us given to us by our Heavenly Father and our brother, Jesus, that is greater than any earthly relationship.

For the sake of our Heavenly Father, due to the size and diversity of our family, can we not put aside our differences, and even our racial and ethnic backgrounds, and love one another the same way that Jesus loves us? He said that's how everyone would know we are His brothers and sisters. Can we not be His "living witnesses" and prove to the cynical world that this divine love with which we are blessed is real?

Think of what a family reunion we are going to have one day when our Heavenly Father calls us all to our heavenly home! All of our redeemed brothers and sisters of the ages will be there in one big glorious bond of divine love that has crossed countless generations and bound us together in one accord as the eternal family of God.

And right in the midst of it all will be a small group of German-Americans named Voss, and old Grandpa Alexander Voss will be looking around in wide-eyed amazement, jumping with joy, and shouting "Das ist gut! Das ist sehr gut!"

Memorial Day

Words fascinate me. As a writer, I'm drawn to their inherent power to enliven thoughts and emotions. A single word, such as "freedom," can unleash the human mind's unlimited imagination; but a single word can also capture and confine your mind and demand a deeper understanding of the word's meaning. "Memorial" is such a word.

A memorial is something that is done or erected as an ongoing reminder befitting a former event. Thus, we designate Memorial Day as a reminder of the hundreds of thousands of Americans who have given their life to protect the freedoms we cherish.

But, is that enough? Is one day out of the year a fitting reminder of their sacrifice? Is a granite stone, a statue, or a wall full of names sufficient? What really is the most meaningful thing that we each can do to honor the lives and sacrifices of those who have died in defense of our freedom?

I have an unusual suggestion. Find a copy of Abraham Lincoln's Gettysburg Address and slowly and carefully read it. You may have never realized this, but President Lincoln dedicated two things on that November day in 1863. First, he dedicated a portion of the great battlefield as "a final resting place for those who here gave their lives that that nation might live."

But there was a second and more transcending dedication. As the great president so eloquently stated, "...it is for us the living, rather, to be dedicated here to the unfinished work which they who fought here have thus far so nobly advanced...that from these honored dead we take increased devotion to that cause for which they gave the last full measure of devotion—that we here highly resolve that these dead shall not have died in vain—that this nation shall have a new birth of freedom and that government of the people, by the people, for the people, shall not perish from the earth."

We focus so little on the second part of Mr. Lincoln's dedication and mostly think that he dedicated a cemetery for the dead at Gettysburg. Indeed, he did, but more importantly, he dedicated a nation of the living to the cause for which those men died in order for America to experience a rebirth of freedom. Mr. Lincoln saw the dedication of the living as the most fitting memorial that could be presented in honor of those who had fallen.

With great compassion, he dedicated the cemetery of the dead. But, with greater and more steadfast passion, he dedicated the nation of the living as a memorial to them.

What if we actually believed Mr. Lincoln's words? When I try to grasp the boundless meaning of freedom, I am compelled to wonder how America would change if we each sincerely rededicated ourselves, with equal courage, commitment, and sacrifice (and using Lincoln's words) to the cause that hundreds of thousands of dead American soldiers "have thus far so notably advanced"? What kind of new birth of freedom might we experience if every American citizen made their life a living memorial to the sacrifice of every dead American soldier? It can be done, but only through personal commitment to the highest calling of citizenship.

May we each bow our head before Almighty God and "highly resolve" that these thousands of dead American soldiers shall not have died in vain, and that each of us will exercise every right of our citizenship to ensure that "life, liberty, and the pursuit of happiness" continues to be the God-given, inalienable right of every American. May we resolve that, in honor of these fallen dead, we will not fail to vote and voice our opinion, and that we will personally take "increased devotion" to truly making America one nation under God with liberty and justice for all. That is the surest way we can guarantee that "government of the people, by the people, for the people, will not perish from the earth."

If we, the living, have the courage and commitment to honor our fallen dead in this way, Memorial Day will truly bring about a new birth of freedom for America.

Kicking up Some Dust

Jesus' disciples had been arguing over who among them would be greatest in the kingdom, and many had already picked out their preferred position of power they hoped to occupy when Jesus proclaimed His messianic kingdom. They all thought His kingdom would be a physical restoration of political and military power, thus making Israel great again. They never understood what Jesus meant by saying, "The kingdom of God is within you."

Their attitude was haughty. Instead, Jesus wanted to teach the disciples about humility, and so He said, "If anyone desires to be first, he shall be last of all and servant of all." It was the exact opposite of what they wanted to hear, and it still is for many today.

We are not called to impose our religious beliefs on others through political power. Rather, we are called to reveal the indiscriminate love of Christ for all people by being their servant. It's quite a reversal of roles, and many so- called Christians aren't one bit interested.

The New Testament often uses the word *diakonos* to describe a servant. It is the concept behind "deacon." I don't mean the "board of directors" deacons of a local church, but the original deacons who humbly busied themselves caring for the needy and providing them with food.

One of the root meanings of *diakonos* is "dust," implying that the servant of Jesus is so busy serving others that he literally kicks up dust in the process of his service to Christ. That is an amazing image to me. Rather than the lazy, complaining, indifferent, judgmental, pious, finger-pointing, front-pew person who feels called by God to point out the faults of others, Jesus said the greatest in the kingdom of heaven—the one who internally experiences God's love for all people the most—is the servant of all who so faithfully works that he kicks up dust helping and serving others.

Have you seen a dust cloud over any churches lately?

For a few days of this coming week, I'm going to get on my knees in the heat of a Mississippi July day and pick cucumbers for an elderly black lady so she can make herself some pickles. For years, she has faithfully helped others, and it's the least I can do to help her. I may not kick up much dust on my knees with an aching back, but for a brief time I'm going to become her servant. Maybe it's just because that's what Jesus told me to do, but the opportunity to serve her is spiritually liberating.

The All-Day Singing

Coaltown Baptist Church, located just down the road, is having their annual Singing School prior to the all-day singing. It's a tradition that is seventy- five to eighty years old and brings back special memories for me.

It's a Southern tradition now largely lost. Music publishing companies would introduce new songs, and local "singing conventions" would then conduct singing schools to learn the new music, plus how to better sing hymns in general, followed by an all-day singing held at a host church.

In those days, the old wood-framed Good Hope Baptist Church hosted the singing school and singing. Held on the third Sunday in June, it was the social event of the season for our community. There was always a big crowd, the windows were opened, people who could not find a seat inside stood outside the windows and doors and sang, and the spirit of fellowship and worship was real. With no air conditioning, wood-handled funeral home fans were plentiful, and singers fanned and sang in harmony.

But the big enjoyment occurred at lunch when dinner was served. If you've ever heard the expression of an "all-day singing with dinner on the ground," this is where it happened. Good Hope had several large red oak trees in the church yard, and wooden frames covered with chicken wire were built under the trees. They were covered in fried chicken, dumplings, every vegetable imaginable—and usually fresh out of the garden—and an abundance of biscuits, cornbread, pies and cakes.

The coffee was made by building a fire around a black wash pot, and the coffee grounds were tied in a flour sack and dropped in the hot water. One year, this mean ole boy from Purvis put a handful of dirt in the pot as a prank when no one was looking, but the coffee was so strong nobody noticed. Usually, somebody stopped by the ice house and brought a few blocks of ice for tea, and chunks of ice were broken loose with a hammer and ice pick.

Most folks ate as though they were starving, and some might nearly have been, and then they walked around saying "Lord have mercy, I ate too much. I don't know how I'm gonna sing this afternoon." Mr. Boleware, an annual visitor, would eat so many dumplings he would take out his false teeth and wipe them off on the rag he had to wipe sweat from his face, and then go back for another helping. He ate like it was the only good meal he had all year—and it might well have been. I was told that he lived alone in a warehouse in Hattiesburg used by a hardware company, and he loved attending singings for both the fellowship and the food.

There were no indoor restrooms, and the one outhouse in the back of the churchyard was a busy place. No one complained; it was all we had.

Were those "good old days"? Well, yes and no. There was definitely a greater sense of community, but over the years in the ministry, I grew fond of air conditioning, good sound systems, tuned pianos, and indoor restrooms.

But I miss watching my mama cook all Sunday morning for the singing, and I miss cleaning out the banana pudding pot with a spoon after she made the pudding. I always hoped there'd be some left after the singing that we could bring home, but Mr. Boleware usually made sure the bowl was empty. I hope he got his fill of mama's banana pudding, because I surely didn't.

Oh, the precious memories that flood my soul.

New Mercy Every Morning

These words of encouragement are for those facing the uncertainty of the week ahead. The Book of Lamentations is a funeral dirge or lament over devastated Jerusalem, a once-thriving city. The destruction, death, and despair that Jeremiah saw moved him to tears.

The first verse of Lamentations reveals the catastrophe that had befallen the people. It should be read slowly and somberly, as one would read a funeral poem: "How lonely sits the city that once was full of people. How like a widow is she, who was once great among the nations!"

Throughout America today, people are struggling with fear and uncertainty, whether caused by economic insecurity, health issues, or the ever-present bickering of political leaders who focus more on themselves and their party than on us. The invading Babylonian army brought emptiness to Jerusalem; uncertainty is our invading enemy. But it leaves us with the same gnawing hunger for truth, clarity, and honesty from leaders who swore on their sacred oath, with God's help, to provide for our common good, if we would just trust them. Ladies and gentlemen, we are eagerly waiting to see your concern and compassion at work, not your polished promises and party talking points.

Maybe we just need to be like Jeremiah. Through his tears, Jeremiah found the hope and courage to face each day, for he declared, "Through the Lord's mercies we are not consumed, because His compassions fail not. They are new every morning; great is Your faithfulness."

This verse became the basis of the great old hymn, "Great is Thy Faithfulness":

> "Great is Thy faithfulness, Oh God, my Father.
> There is no shadow of turning with Thee.
> Thou changest not, Thy compassions they fail not,
> As Thou has been, Thou forever will be.
> Great is Thy faithfulness, Great is Thy faithfulness,
> Morning by morning new mercies I see.
> All I have needed Thy hand hath provided,
> Great is Thy faithfulness Lord unto me."

As we together face the economic and political challenges touching our land and sadly look at all the businesses, streets, and cities that once were full of confident, thriving people, you can faithfully cling to God's promises Jeremiah echoed: "Through the Lord's mercies we are not consumed. Because His compassions fail not, they are new every morning "

You may be viewing the circumstances around you this morning through the tears of despair, just as Jeremiah did. But I assure you that you can also see something else "morning by morning new mercies I see." Because His compassion never fails, you can face each day with hope. His word assures us, "Through the Lord's mercies we are not consumed," and you will see evidence of that morning, by morning, by morning....

Lessons Learned from a Plague

The Sign and Wonder of a Burning Bush

The critical moment in Moses' divine call occurred when he came to Horeb, the mountain of God, and saw a burning bush that wasn't consumed by the fire, with the Angel of the Lord standing in the flames. Although Moses saw this "great sight" with his physical eyes, God gave him spiritual insight about the deeper meaning of the amazing view he beheld.

Throughout the Bible, God uniquely works through "signs and wonders," which are essentially two separate ways of seeing the same event. Certain physical occurrences that were completely beyond human capability were viewed as a sign from God and as something only He could do, thus leaving one filled with awe, amazement, and wonder at God's holiness and power. The first few chapters of Acts, for example, contain several references to signs and wonders that powerfully inspired the early Christian church. The only appropriate reaction to such an event is humbling oneself before God in worship and obedience.

It is safe to say that standing before a burning bush that the fire did not consume had this impact on Moses. In fact, God told Moses that his ability to bring the Israelites back to Mount Horeb and worship would be a sign that God was with him in his divine mission. God further told Moses that He would "stretch out My hand and strike Egypt with all My wonders which I will do in its midst "Clearly, the plagues on Egypt, leading to the Israelite escape from enslavement, falls in the category of "signs and wonders."

As Moses viewed the burning bush, he heard the voice of God telling him to remove his sandals from his feet as a gesture of reverence and worship, "for the place where you stand is holy ground."

Moses knew the experience before him would reveal God's power and holiness in ways he could not envision, leaving all future generations marveling in awe and wonder. Indeed, that became true.

Are we Americans not standing in front of a burning bush today? In my seventy-five years, I've lived through several political and economic crises in this country. But no one would have convinced me I would see the day when America essentially went into lockdown and virtually ceased to function. We boastfully state that we are the most powerful nation in the world, yet God has taken a microscopic virus and brought us to our knees. No human power could do this, but God can as a sign of His divine power, leaving each of us in awe and wonder at what is occurring in our nation.

If we are willing to view this pandemic through spiritual eyes as a sign and wonder from God, rather than just complaining about the physical and economic impact, we can experience the same truth and inspiration that Moses realized.

God told Moses, "I will certainly be with you," and the same is true for each of us. Regardless of what you are experiencing in this crisis, God is with you. In the days ahead, you may experience His power, protection, and providence in ways that will leave you in awe and wonder.

The existence and extent of this virus is not just some freakish biological event that we bemoan. The journey on which God will lead us can become holy ground divinely created for us to journey into a greater understanding of God's holiness and power than we have ever known. If we will walk this holy path with Him, God will lead us to a realm of faith and worship that will bring revival and spiritual renewal to America.

Even as Moses saw that the fire did not destroy the bush (a symbol of God's holiness), we, too, will prevail and endure because of God's presence with us. He does not wish to destroy us; rather, God desires to purify us with the fire of His holiness from the sin and spiritual indifference that has too long plagued America.

What is His Name?

"Indeed, when I come to the children of Israel and say to them, 'The God of your fathers has sent me to you,' and they say to me, 'What is His name?' what shall I say to them?'" (Exod. 3:13).

It is one of the most spiritually heart-wrenching questions in the Bible and reveals the consequence of a centuries-old drift away from God. What lessons can we learn from the question, "What shall I tell them Your name is?" Interestingly, Moses did not know the name and nature of God either, or he wouldn't have asked the question, yet he was so profoundly impacted by the sign and wonder of the burning bush that he faithfully and willingly obeyed.

We learn from this question how easily God's people can get caught up in worldly circumstances and forget God's holiness and His presence in their lives. The "children of Israel" were Jacob's descendants. Their forefathers had journeyed into Egypt centuries before as nothing but starving, impoverished shepherds searching for food and a place for their flocks to graze. But God had made a covenant promise to bless them, and they were allowed to remain in Egypt and, through the intercession of Joseph, were permitted to live in Goshen, one of the most fertile and productive regions of Egypt. There, they prospered and grew into a "mighty nation."

Sadly, a spiritual cancer was also growing within them. Over the span of four hundred years, while they grew prosperous and strong, they stopped worshiping God. Gone were the memories of His providence; gone were the memories of how God used Joseph to place them in one of the most beautiful and bountiful places on Earth; gone were memories of God's covenant promises to their forefathers, Abraham, Isaac, and Jacob; and gone was any concept of themselves as God's special people.

Instead, they had surrendered their sense of holiness to God to the gods of Egypt and had become a part of the pagan culture around them. Wealth, power, and pleasure slowly became their dominant interests—their gods.

Moses knew this to be true. He knew that when he called them to have faith and trust in the God of their fathers, they would have virtually no idea who he was talking about. They would neither know His name nor know anything about Him. So, Moses asked God this sobering question, "Who are You? Who will I tell them You are?"

I am deeply concerned that we here in America have followed in their footsteps. We have forgotten what a divine miracle America really is. We no longer teach how God took a band of pilgrims and grew them into the most powerful nation in the world. In our prideful arrogance, we now believe we did it ourselves.

We no longer tell our children about the numerous times Americans hopelessly had their back to the wall in battle and were miraculously delivered. Most people today are clueless about how God answered George Washington's ceaseless prayers for food for his starving army in the snow and bitter cold at Valley Forge. The list of miracles by the God of our fathers is endless, but most today know nothing about them and have no interest.

Instead, the gods of pleasure, greed, wealth, and the obsession to be cool, trendy, and accepted by flashing around the latest fads, fashion, tattoos, gadgets, and cool talk is more important. For many Americans, the latest model iPhone and its features is far more important than a personal knowledge of the God of their fathers.

If you were to ask a random sample of Americans to describe the God who blessed their forefathers with the strength, wisdom, and courage to establish the United States of America, most would be clueless. They wouldn't know enough to even ask, "What is His name?"

And you wonder why a microscopic virus is being divinely used to bring us to our knees and open our eyes. We can learn some transforming lessons of spiritual truth from a plague, if we will stop complaining and pointing the finger of blame and instead pray for wisdom, insight, and the courage of spiritual obedience.

"I AM WHO I AM"
(A monologue sermon)

"My name is Moses. You probably have read about how I led the Israelites out of Egyptian bondage toward the Promised Land following all the plagues, and you may think of me as some great spiritual leader that gave God's people the Ten Commandments. God has used me, and I'm humbled by that. But it was a different story at the beginning, and I'd like to tell you about my early struggle.

I was running for my life because I had killed an Egyptian who had attacked a fellow Israelite, and I knew what would happen to me if I was caught. I can't tell you how scared I was. Everything in my life was in turmoil. And it was almost the same for my people. For years we had prospered in Goshen, a fertile area in Egypt. But a new Pharoah had appointed taskmasters over us and made slaves of us. Everything we had known was now on the verge of being destroyed. People's jobs, their homes, farms, and businesses were being lost and destroyed.

Throughout the land, there was panic, anxiety, worry, and you could hear people groaning not only over their fear of losing everything they had worked for, but there was a pervasive fear of death. It just seemed that suddenly a great catastrophe had swept over us, and we struggled under the burdens now facing us—physical and financial burdens we had never known before. There was so much change happening in both my own life and in the life of my people that we literally did not know what tomorrow would bring. There was a terror and dread slowly sweeping over the land, and no one knew what to do.

It was in the midst of this overwhelming fear and uncertainty that I had a life-changing experience with God in front of a burning bush. When He told me to go tell my people that God would deliver them from the fear and anxiety of the bondage that now gripped them, I first had to ask God to tell me His name. He answered me in a way that changed my understanding of God and transformed my faith in Him.

It wasn't like another man's voice that spoke to me. Instead, it was like a quiet inner voice that made me think about the overwhelming fear, uncertainty, and change that my people and I faced compared to God's unchanging nature. In Egypt, the gods people worshipped were always changing, whether it was their political leader, their wealth, their prestige and power, or one of the many natural gods people dreamed up. People could create a new god for any occasion, and they were always changing. I knew that no one would really follow and worship some fickle god of change. They would just pretend and make a mockery of faith.

But I sensed something far different about the God of my fathers. He was unchanging. The more I compared His nature to the unpredictable and unreliable gods invented by man, the more I saw His holy nature and His pure and perfect ways.

This quiet voice within me whispered and said, "His name is 'I AM.'" He is who He is, and there are no other man-made gods on Earth like Him.

Then I realized something even greater about His name and His nature. If He is who He is today, and He is unchanging, then He has always been who He is, and He will always be who He is. I realized that His name is I AM WHO I AM. He quietly spoke to me, "I AM the same today as I was yesterday and the same as I will be tomorrow. You never have to worry about Me changing into some unknown, unreliable, and unpredictable god like those you have known in this land of bondage."

I pondered the meaning of that in my mind, and I realized that God was telling me that He will repeatedly be the same God in the future that He has consistently been in the past. It was as if He was assuring me that He will forever be who He is now and who He has always been. He is the one eternally unchanging God.

I can't describe the calm and peace that I experienced. In the midst of all the fear, uncertainty, and anxiety we faced, here was the one sure thing we could cling to and use as a spiritual anchor in the turmoil around us—the unchanging nature of the God of our fathers who loved us and wanted to deliver us to a land filled with His promises. I realized that the name and nature of God is I AM WHO I AM. There are no additions or subtractions to God's nature and no surprises or disappointments. He is the one true constant on whom I can depend.

If He is the God who made a covenant promise to my fathers, then He is the one God I can trust today to fulfill that promise tomorrow. If He was the God who created the heavens and the Earth yesterday, then He is the God who holds all forces of nature in His hand today and will deliver His people tomorrow. If He lovingly placed Adam and Eve in the Garden of Eden yesterday, and placed us in the Land of Goshen today, then the Promised Land of tomorrow will be even better.

He has never cursed us with less; He has always blessed us with more, and He will continue to do so. In the journey before us, He may pull down some of the pagan gods we have worshiped, but in doing so, He will open our eyes to the amazing truth of His constant, unchanging love for us.

You may also be faced with fear, anxiety, and uncertainty in your life today, and people around you may be turning to some weak and constantly changing god in hope of deliverance. It will not work. Those gods invented by man are powerless and pagan.

The greatest spiritual reality you can experience—one that will give you the strength to face your fear of today and the uncertainty of tomorrow—is to realize the unchanging nature of Holy God. He will continue to be the all-powerful loving God that He has always been. When all else is falling apart around you, in Him and in His unchanging nature you can place your faith. He will not fail you. He can deliver you from whatever you face.

Your fellow servant of the great I AM   Moses."

When This is Over and Things Get Back to Normal

I've often wondered why there were ten plagues that hit Egypt before the

Israelites were finally free. Some Bible scholars suggest that God brought judgment on every pagan God worshiped by the Egyptians, while others say the number represents the totality of divine judgment. A combination of both is probably more accurate.

The attitude of many people today has given me another understanding. Could it be that, at every stage of the plagues on Egypt, the Egyptian leader assured the people that everything was under control and that circumstances would soon improve and not worsen? Is it possible that after each plague, the general consensus was, "When this is over and everything returns to normal, we'll be ok"? Nowhere in the biblical account does anyone suggest that "the worst may yet be ahead of us, and we really have no idea what may come next."

Even as conditions progressively worsened, Pharoah showed no willingness to recognize the supreme power of God. Amazingly, after the death angel brought untold suffering and countless deaths, Pharoah still defiantly pursued the fleeing Israelites into the waters of the Red Sea. He never acknowledged that God was greater and more powerful than he was, and that attitude tragically brought disaster upon his land.

Have you ever pondered why Pharoah's heart was "hardened" and he refused to free the Israelites. Consider this: The number of Israelites was over 100,000 (some have argued it was as high as 400,000), and if the majority of them were tasked as slaves with making bricks, that would produce hundreds of thousands of bricks at no cost for Pharoah's building projects. Could it be that Pharoah knew the economic hit he would suffer by letting these people go? Did Pharoah coldly calculate the potential economic cost of obeying God and defiantly decided that obedience was too costly?

Some in this country seem to have a similar attitude about this virus. I've read news accounts about its predicted peak and when it might end, and it's the same "when this is over and everything returns to normal" attitude. "We can deal with this, and things will soon be ok again" seems to be a prevalent attitude of hope. But, honestly, is that a realistic attitude?

I personally hope that it does end soon. But I've had a feeling from the beginning that this is a once-in-a-lifetime experience where each of us, and America as a whole, confronts God in front of a burning bush, and we are compelled to view the impact of this virus as a sign and wonder from God that overwhelmingly reveals how powerful and holy God is and how weak and vulnerable we are.

What will it take for us to finally see this as a sign and wonder from God and not only remove the proverbial sandals from our feet as an act of worship and submission, but also realize this is holy ground on which we are standing and the journey we are on is divinely ordained to get us all back into a closer relationship with God?

I am amazed by what God used to bring down mighty Pharoah. He could have armed the Israelites militarily, since they had grown into "a mighty nation" in the area of Goshen, but God chose to use means to defeat the mighty Egyptian nation through which only He could be gloried, and people would view His actions with awe and wonder.

Rather than making a "David versus Goliath" out of every Hebrew male and empowering them to victoriously fight for their freedom, God first used what some have suggested was red algae to turn the fresh water of rivers as red as blood, including water in buckets and pitchers, so that it became putrid and undrinkable. People frantically dug holes in the river banks searching for fresh water. This was followed by an invasion of frogs, then lice that tortured both man and beast. Next came huge swarms of flies followed by pestilence that killed livestock throughout Egypt.

After this, people and animals became infected with painful boils and open sores on their bodies. Then came violent weather storms producing hail of a magnitude never seen before. Once the disastrous weather had subsided, swarms of locusts swept over the land devouring trees and plants not destroyed by the hail. And yet after each one, there was the same defiant "when this is over and everything gets back to normal" attitude. Even the nation-wide grieving over unprecedented death rates didn't change Pharoah's heart.

Our President said a few days ago that we will have done a good job if we can hold the final death toll to 100,000 people. That's mindboggling, and yet there remains an attitude among our highest leadership that when we've reached that point and everything returns to normal, we'll be ok.

But, can we safely assume that? Many Christians have long prayed for a spiritual awakening in America. I don't want to sound like a prophet of doom, but we should realistically view this plague as a sign and wonder from God in which He brings the richest and most powerful nation in the world to her knees with a microscopic virus.

In my humble opinion, Covid is not simply a freakish biological outbreak. In answer to countless prayers for a spiritual awakening, God has brought

America before a burning bush. This virus and its impact is a sign and wonder from God. Nothing remotely approaching the potential consequences of this plague has ever struck this nation. If this is God's purpose in this plague, then we truly have no idea what blights of flies, frogs, lice, locusts, and hailstorms await us until we humble ourselves under the mighty hand of God.

The sooner we see this as a sign and wonder from God and recommit ourselves through true spiritual repentance—and not just political posturing and lip service—to the Christian ideals on which America was founded, and we worship and love God with all our heart, mind, and soul and love our neighbors as ourselves free from judgmental condemnation of others unlike us, the sooner this modern-day plague will end.

I believe that every Christian ought to humble themselves in front of this burning bush, as did Moses, and fervently ask God to protect us, provide for us, and preserve us until the death angel has passed over us and we are free of this plague and God has accomplished His perfect will and brought revival and a spiritual awakening to our troubled land.

We do not know what tomorrow holds, but praise God, we know who holds tomorrow. And so, as Christians we can say with firm faith, "When this is over and things get back to normal, we will be ok."

Blood on the Doorpost

The final plague God unleashed on Egypt as a sign and wonder was a night of unprecedented terror for the Egyptians. We don't know exactly how it happened or how long it lasted. The Bible succinctly describes how God's warrior angel brought death at midnight to the firstborn in every Egyptian home, including Pharoah's. The wails of grief, despair, and fear echoed through the night.

The visitation of the death angel was an overwhelming sign of God's power to judge, but God revealed another sign and wonder in that night of terror that would forever serve as a historical underpinning for both the Jewish and Christian faiths. It was the sign of the blood on the doorpost of every Hebrew home.

The Israelites were instructed to kill a sacrificial lamb and sprinkle some of the blood on their doorposts. On seeing the blood of the lamb, the death angel would pass over that home and not bring the plague of death on it.

As God's judgment unfolded, there were the sad cries of the condemned and the shouts of praise of deliverance from those covered by the blood of the lamb. From that night forward, the celebration of Passover became a cornerstone of both the Jewish and Christian faith in recognition of God's mercy.

The ancient Jewish calendar was based on cycles of the moon. The year began with the spring equinox (when days and nights are the same length) and the new moon that followed. Two weeks later was the celebration of Passover, and it occurred during the full moon. Jesus was crucified on Friday before the Passover Sabbath. When He arose from death on Sunday morning, the celebration of Easter was forever set as the first Sunday after the first full moon following the spring equinox.

In our Christian emphasis on Easter and Jesus' resurrection, we often overlook the ancient meaning of Passover to our Christian faith. But Passover establishes the fundamental principle that it is the blood of the Sacrificial Lamb on the doorpost of our life that enables us to escape the judgment of death. Our Lamb is Jesus, and it is His blood on our life that covers our sin and assures us the gift of everlasting life through His resurrection and through our faith in Him. When Jesus sacrificed His life on the cross in atonement for our sin, He became God's eternal Passover lamb.

If you need a reason to shout for joy in the midst of the pain, suffering, and death around us, celebrate your own ancient Passover and know that, because of Jesus' blood on the doorpost of your life, death has forever forfeited its claim on you and will forever pass over you. For through the power of Jesus' death and resurrection, you have entered into His everlasting life. There is no greater sign and wonder of God's love for you.

Confronting Fear

In his first inaugural address on March 4, 1933, President Franklin Roosevelt spoke to a nation gripped in an unprecedented and uncontrollable crisis. With wisdom and insight, FDR focused on the greatest obstacle to a sensible program of recovery—fear. Americans, Roosevelt reasoned, could formulate plans and programs to address the problems facing the nation, but there was no real answer for nationwide fear and panic. People were afraid and fearful of losing their jobs, farms, and homes. But they were also fearful of government programs, control, and intrusion into their lives.

Until a sense of calm was restored and common sense prevailed, Roosevelt knew the crisis would continue. Thus, this wise leader intoned these inspired words of wisdom to his troubled people: "...the only thing we have to fear is fear itself." Mr. Roosevelt's words ring clear again today.

Fear is an unseen enemy of the worst kind. It can attack an individual or an entire nation without warning, rendering logic useless, restraint ineffective, and pleas for reason heedless. It is the fertile soil in which panic matures into hysteria. Until fear subsides, reason will never bear fruit.

Fear almost always produces a personal reaction that falls into observable categories. There is the rational reaction to a known danger (I don't go near a snake); the irrational reaction to a known danger (I see a snake in my driveway from my window, and I start screaming and lock the doors); the rational reaction to an unknown danger (I don't know if the snake is there, but I walk cautiously in areas where he may be hiding); and the irrational reaction to an unknown danger (I don't know if there's a snake in my yard, but I stay inside fearfully crying at the thought that it might be).

Somewhere in these is our personal reaction to this present crisis. We can either use common sense and reasonably react to the known danger, or we can irrationally react to the unknown danger the virus poses and lapse into senseless behavior, or even hysteria. However, before any effective nationwide plan can be implemented, the American people must first learn to reasonably and sensibly react to what is known about the dangers of this virus and stop panic buying, spreading rumors and ridiculous conspiracy theories, and acting with a mob mentality.

Each of us—all of us—and America as a whole is sailing apprehensively in uncharted waters. We've never been here before; we've never faced such sheer uncertainty. We have no idea what this virus may cause. It may rapidly disappear, or it may spread uncontrollably and kill multiple thousands, leaving our beloved nation devastated. We all should be prudently cautious and concerned.

In these uncertain days, we must each assume a role of leadership, whether it is within our family reassuring worried children, or as teachers caring for disrupted students, or community leaders speaking calmly and reassuringly, or overworked healthcare workers caring for and consoling sick patients and those scared of dying. Valor is the courageous act of common people in a dangerous and uncommon situation caring for others ahead of themselves. We need that now.

Am I personally fearful? At first, I wasn't, but reality has come home to roost. I'm over seventy years old with chronic heart disease, respiratory weakness, and a history of pneumonia. I am among the most vulnerable, so look for me in either the "rational reaction to a known danger" or the "rational reaction to an unknown danger" category.

Each of us must use the common-sense God gave us and exercise reason and responsibility as never before. We must become good stewards of practicality, prudence, and protection, thus setting an example for others. All of us, in our own small way, must respond to the holy calling of crisis leadership.

What defines leadership for me (and we must all see the responsibility of our individual influence on others) is not our ability to come up with ingenious plans, but rather our individual ability to overcome our own fear and instill courage and confidence in those looking to us in trust for guidance and encouragement. We can meet that challenge, and with calm resolve and unwavering faith in God, we can victoriously work through this crisis.

Interestingly, fear plays an important role in biblical history. Realize that the Judeo-Christian faith is premised on people first coming to grips with their fear: Mary was fearful of being unmarried and pregnant, which might get her stoned to death; the shepherds were gripped in fear at the appearance of the angelic messengers; and the disciples were fearful of being left without Jesus being personally with them. Even Jesus fearfully agonized over going to the cross.

But the fear that Moses had to overcome in leading God's people out of Egyptian enslavement defies our comprehension. He had no credentials as a leader, no plan or strategy, and no clear answer to what the future held. He had killed an Egyptian, and he was running for his life. In short, he had no idea what he was doing or what he was going to do.

For him to confront Pharoah, with all of his power, and demand freedom and release for the Hebrew people would be viewed as an insane act inviting certain death. But he found the courage to do so, and he prevailed through the power of God. Moses became one of the greatest leaders in history only after he dealt with his fear.

But you may be wondering, how does this virus relate to the plagues that hit Egypt centuries ago? Is there a thread of commonality? Yes, and it's found in a most unlikely place. Have you ever wondered where Moses learned to overcome his paralyzing fear? He learned it in a transforming moment standing in front of a burning bush that was not consumed by the fire, and he was never again the same. Perhaps each of us needs to stand there also and confront our own fear.

You may not realize this, but America may be about to have her own burning bush experience, and the lessons of faith God will teach us in the days ahead through the plague of this virus might transform us also, even as it did Moses and the Israelites.

We've Crossed Over

The miraculous parting of the Red Sea is one of the most mysterious events in history. Surely, it was an amazing sign and wonder from God for the Israelites fleeing Pharoah's pursuing army, for it divinely provided them a safe way to cross over to the other side. Pharoah's army falsely presumed that, if the sea would part for the Israelites, it would surely remain parted for them, and onto the dry seabed floor they stormed, only to be engulfed by the water cascading down on them. The Israelites, once toiling in bondage, crossed over and were now safe and free on the other side. Their new life, given to them by the mercy and grace God, had begun.

Are there similarities between the experience of the Israelites crossing over the Red Sea and our spiritual journey as Christians? Yes, and it is a powerful testimony to Jesus and His singular ability to take us to a new dimension and experience of life.

When Jesus came forth from the tomb of death, alive ever more, He brought you with Him, if you have faith in Him as a Christian. Because of His resurrection, you must grasp the amazing truth that, just like crossing the Red Sea, you've crossed over to the other side.

You've left behind the fear and uncertainty of the spiritual and physical bondage in which you've been enslaved, and you've entered into a heavenly experience of life divinely created for you since the beginning of time. You have experienced the mercy of His death on the cross; now you powerfully live in the grace of His resurrection, for you have passed from death into everlasting life. You've crossed over to the other side, and your life will never again be the same.

Rejoice, you're not enslaved any longer! The terrible toll sin has taken on your life is behind you. You've crossed over into a life of freedom. Christ has personally set you free, and you will never be in bondage again. Shout "hallelujah," for you have crossed over from a life filled with burdens and despair into a daily walk with God filled with unexplainable miracles, grace, and mercy that you will experience fresh and new each day.

Let your "Amen" ring to the mountaintop, for you've crossed over into a divine realm where the presence of God is constantly with you day and night. In your covenant relationship with Jesus, He will never leave you, and you will see evidence of His presence each day, as if the Holy Spirit were a cloud overshadowing you by day and a pillar of fire guiding you by night.

Glory be to God, you've crossed over into an experience with the Lord where bitter water becomes sweet water constantly quenching your thirst for His righteousness, and manna from heaven freely falls on you each day, filling you with spiritual nourishment and giving you strength to gloriously live for Him. Through the bread of life and the living water that only Christ provides, you shall be eternally filled and your soul satisfied.

Praise His holy name, you've crossed over into a journey with God where He will lead you into a realm of faith in which, through Christ, He will fulfill every divine promise that He ever made to you, and He will never leave you spiritually empty and unfulfilled.

Lift your hands in praise, for you've crossed over and, though you are still in this world, you are not a part of it. Your citizenship now is in heaven, and you now gladly set your eyes on the things that are above and not on the things of this world.

With tears of joy on your face, realize that you've crossed over from spiritual poverty into being an adopted child of God and a joint-heir with Christ to all the blessings and riches of God's heavenly kingdom.

Praise Him, for you've crossed over to a land where you can cease your burdensome labors and enter into His rest. Lift your bowed head, bent low by the burdens and despair you have known, and get a sparkle back in your eyes. Let a smile come on your face that hasn't been there in a long while, and break forth in a hymn of joy. You're not toiling in your own Egyptian bondage any more—you've crossed over to the other side!

Don't look back. The old things have passed away, and all things have become new. You've been reborn into a life you never imagined. There are no plagues any more. Death has lost its sting, the grave has lost its victory, and you have become immortal. You're now a disciple of Jesus, you are filled with Holy Spirit power, and you've commenced your eternal journey with Him. Ten thousand years from now it will still be as fresh and powerful as if it had just begun.

Jump with heavenly joy if you want to, for the prison bars of Egypt in your life have been slammed shut through the power of Jesus' resurrection, and you have crossed over to the other side—redeemed, free, and eternally alive in Christ in His heavenly kingdom for all the ages to come. The resurrection of Jesus has completely changed the focus and priorities of your life from this burdensome world to the bliss of the kingdom of heaven.

Praise God Almighty, through the power of Jesus' resurrection, the waters of the sea of despair have parted, the stone has been rolled away, and our resurrected Lord has gathered us up in His loving arms and carried us safe to the other side. That's what makes this day such a glorious experience— we've crossed over to the other side!

New Eyes for Her Son and
One Grateful Mother

(John 9:1-34)

She must have been speechless, as were many others. The change in her blind and facially disfigured son was so dramatic that he was nearly unrecognizable, even by family and friends who knew him. He had been unmercifully shunned, shamed, and condemned as a sinner by religious zealots because of his blindness, and they even included his parents in their condemnation.

But Jesus saw this poor helpless beggar differently. He saw him as an opportunity to glorify the miraculous mercy of God, even if He had to violate cold, unyielding religious law to do so, and He also saw a man who would spend the rest of his life thanking and praising God for his healing.

It was the Sabbath, and Jesus knew the law forbade healing on that holy day, but His compassion and mercy for this poor man compelled Him to help him and heal him. Jesus spat on the ground and made mud with which He anointed the blind man's eyes. He then told him to go wash in the Pool of Siloam, and as he did, he was healed.

This poor man wasn't just healed, he was mercifully and miraculously transformed, as if he were made into a new person. I personally believe that Jesus made him new eyes with the miracle mud, and that's why his appearance was so remarkably different. Can you even begin to imagine his mother's joy on seeing her restored son, and can you imagine his joy in seeing his mother for the first time? It was a Sabbath that joyful mother celebrated for the rest of her life.

In stark contrast, the religious purists saw this miracle of healing as a sin against God because it was done on the Sabbath. Confronting and again condemning the healed man, the Pharisees emphatically called Jesus a sinner and said that He could not possibly be a Man of God because He healed and transformed this blind man's life on the Sabbath, which to them was unlawful labor.

When the man insisted it was Jesus who healed him, they excommunicated the young man from his religion. It didn't matter, for he now had a merciful Master to worship, Jesus the Son of God.

This mother's gratitude must have been boundless. Since her son's birth, she had struggled with the accusation that her sin, or her husband's sin, caused her child's blindness. That's what the legalists coldly told her. Imagine her burden, her sense of guilt, her ceaseless prayers, and her desperate desire to find just one person who would truly care about her son, and about her also. She found that one person in Jesus and His merciful healing, when all others said it was unlawful for Him to do so.

I have the deepest respect and admiration for godly mothers and the unique blessings they provide through the marvelous ministry of motherhood. Only the Good Lord knows the number of children whose lives have been transformed, and who have a new vision for Christ, solely because of the boundless mercy of God and the unconditional love and ceaseless prayers of a loving mother.

Matthew and Simon:

An Example of Christian Discipleship

I recently read an article stating that the President of the United States called the Governor of Washington a "snake" because of a policy disagreement. I never thought we, as a Christian nation, would see the day when our public discourse is so vitriolic and coarse, and that I would see friends on social media heartily sharing mean-spirited comments about those with whom they disagree. None of this is consistent with the spirit of Christianity.

The Gospels describe an easily overlooked relationship between two antagonists that should serve as an example for us today. It is an amazing demonstration of transformed attitudes through Christian discipleship.

Matthew was a tax collector who contracted with Rome to collect the assessed tax levy in his district. Whatever amount he collected above that levy, through whatever harsh and abusive means he employed, was his to keep as his fee. Rome didn't care what method he used so long as he met their minimum assessment. Through merciless intimidation, many tax collectors became exceedingly rich, such as Zacchaeus, the chief tax collector in the Jericho region.

Tax collectors were viewed as traitors to Israel and were passionately hated, especially by the radical Zealots, a nationalistic political group that openly advocated rebellion against Rome, regardless of the cost.

Simon was a member, and thus he was known as Simon the Zealot. His hatred for Matthew the Roman tax collector would have been extreme. If he could have killed Matthew, Simon would have believed that God would bless him.

Jesus called both Matthew and Simon as disciples, and not by accident. If these two could become Christian brothers without personal bitterness, then anyone could experience the same. It was a brilliant strategic move to prove the power of Christian discipleship, and it worked.

One would think that a gathering of disciples that included these two enemies, seething with hatred, would have resulted in a screaming, cursing display of bitterness, but it never happened. Once they became disciples of

47

Jesus, there is no record of any further animosity between them. Their personal relationship was transformed by their Christian discipleship.

Why can't the same be true for us in this Christian land that is "one nation under God"? If each of us experienced an attitude transformation like that of Simon the Zealot and Matthew the tax collector, maybe Jesus could also use us to prove that Christian discipleship is real.

The Bride

Introduction

Both the Old and New Testaments describe our relationship with God as a covenant. Since a covenant must involve at least two, from the opening chapters of Genesis through the last page of The Revelation, one may find the image, existence, and symbolism of another who enjoys a unique relationship with God, and who may be generally referred to as the Bride, or at least that is how I have come to visualize this other covenant role. In the closing passages of The Revelation, it is both the Spirit and the Bride who plead for Christ's return, and they cry out, "Come!" (Rev. 22:17).

Although she initially appears as Eve, thereafter the Bride is not one person alone, but rather a "nation of people" who are in a unique relationship with God that is the equivalent of a covenant marriage. Interestingly, the Bible then isn't about the actions of God alone, but because of the two-person covenant concept, the response of the second party to the outpouring of God's unmerited love should also be examined and provides a fascinating biblical study. Think of it in this manner: A husband may love his wife dearly and unconditionally, but unless we know how she responds to his love, we don't have a good understanding of their true relationship. Thus, the response of the Bride is very important in understanding the Bible.

In the Old Testament, God's special relationship with Israel is sometimes described as a marriage because it was so close and binding. For example, Hosea, the prophet, portrayed Israel's sinful and defiant attitude toward God as being like his relationship with Gomer, his adulterous wife.

Further, Israel is described in Isaiah 62:4 as the "land of Beulah," which refers to a land of covenant marriage. "Beulah" means married. That is how the prophet saw Israel's relationship with God when she returned to Him in true worship. So, when you hear the great Christian song "Beulah Land," it is not just an odd name for a physical location, but rather a name describing a unique place of divinely blissful covenant marriage. Thus, in order for Israel to be understood as "Beulah Land," she must also be seen in the role of the Bride.

In the New Testament, the redeemed church, those who are bought by the blood of Jesus, occupies this same role with Christ. The Church is referred to as "the called-out ones," and they are called out from the world and set apart through sanctification to live a unique, blessed, and blissful spiritual life as the Bride of Christ.

This eternal union will be celebrated throughout heaven in the Marriage Supper of the Lamb. As a Christian, you will be there, and here's how the Bible describes you on that great day: "...and His wife has made herself ready. And to her it was granted to be arrayed in fine linen, clean and bright, for the fine linen is the righteous acts of the saints" (Rev. 19:7-9). You will be radiant, perfect, pure, and sinless in His sight.

Maybe you have never before envisioned your Christian faith in this manner, but you are a very important part of the Bride of Christ, and you must begin seeing yourself in that unique, personal, and exclusive relationship with Jesus. There can be no greater joy for a bride than the day of her marriage, and it is not the intent of Jesus for that joy to diminish in your life, but rather for it to increase. You may have never thought about it like this, but your relationship with Jesus is a covenant of spiritual marriage, thus making you a member of His redeemed church and a part of the Bride of Christ.

In this holy covenant union, you have no idea of the magnitude of His love for you, His devotion to you, and His commitment to use the fullness of His divine power to purify His Bride and cleanse her of all inequity so "that He might present her to Himself a glorious church, not having spot or wrinkle or any such thing, but that she should be holy and without blemish" (Eph. 5:27).

We can only try to imagine the magnitude of the eternal blessings He has prepared for us within His heavenly kingdom, because "eye has not seen, nor ear heard, nor have entered into the heart of man" what awaits us (1 Cor. 2:9). The more you understand the gift of grace and the eternal blessings reserved only for the Bride since the beginning of time, the greater is your experience and expression of joy, for that is your spiritual inheritance in Him.

You must also understand that the Bride's inheritance is fully vested and not subject to loss, set aside in her name, and guarded and protected by countless legions of heavenly angels. Because you are in a covenant with Jesus, you are listed as a joint-heir with Christ to all the blessings of His heavenly kingdom (Rom. 8:17).

Please, for the glory of Christ and the honor of the Bridegroom, stop cheating yourself out of the joy of your salvation. Your Christian faith is so much more than just joining the church and getting baptized. You are now and forevermore bound to Jesus in a covenant of spiritual marriage that is unbreakable. It is a personal and powerful relationship He has entered into with you. Because the covenant is premised on His unbroken presence, He will never leave you nor forsake you, and He is with you in every circumstance of your life. There is no other in His life, for you are a part of His Bride!

Please start thinking of yourself in this manner, and let your life radiate the joy that only the Bride can know. Dear friend, you are passionately loved!

The Covenant Relationship

Since the Bible portrays God's relationship with man as a covenant akin to spiritual marriage, our understanding of His love for the Bride is greatly enhanced by a deeper understanding of an ancient covenant and its relevance today. Although we primarily think of the two Bible divisions as the old and new covenants, there are other covenants recorded in the Bible, such as God's covenant with Abraham (Gen. 17:2) and another with Moses (Exo. 24:7-8). There are also covenants between individuals, such as David and Jonathan (Read 1 Sam. 18:1-4 for an excellent description of the covenant bond).

A covenant is probably the oldest form of a binding agreement, yet we still find evidence of its influence today, especially in marriage ceremonies. In addition, as we examine the various covenant segments, it is apparent how they represent Jesus' covenant with His Bride, the church, with each of us being a part.

Years ago, I found a description of the basic components of ancient covenants that greatly impacted my understanding of how this agreement ritual helps reveal God's love for us. I have pondered its meaning many times.

A covenant was based on the invitation of one party to another. It was a serious, deeply personal, life-transforming arrangement entered into only with much forethought and commitment. When Jesus said, "Come, follow Me," it is a covenant invitation that totally transforms the life of one who responds.

The covenant partners first exchanged a small piece of personal property, symbolizing that the possessions of each wholly belonged to the other as well, such as Jonathan giving David his robe and personal armor. Although we struggle to truly make Jesus a joint owner of all we have, He nevertheless makes us a joint-heir to all the riches of His heavenly kingdom (Rom. 8:17).

It is a pledge of one to the other that "all that is mine is yours, and all that is yours is mine."

Each took a part of the other's name, symbolizing a common identity, just as a woman today takes her husband's name. Thus, God promises forgiveness and healing, "If My people who are called by My name...will humble themselves and pray..." (2 Chron. 7:14). Jesus became the Son of Man so that He could make each of us a son of God (Gal. 3:26). Christian does not just designate your faith; it denotes your personal identification with Jesus and becomes your personal identity as much as your given name.

Each made a small cut on their body, indicating they belonged exclusively to another, and swapped a drop of blood indicating the two lives were now one and separable only by death. Thus, it became a blood covenant, the most binding form of an agreement. "Cutting a covenant" was an ancient description, and Jewish male circumcision is the primary Old Testament example. In the New Testament, the Apostle Paul describes this as a "circumcision of the heart," denoting a Christian's blood covenant with Jesus (Rom. 2:29).

When Jesus said "this...is the new covenant in My blood," He made a vow to you that few stop to ponder. The blood of one was believed to cover over the life of the other, so that the life of each was primarily visible in the other. That is the basis of blood atonement. The blood of Jesus shed on the cross covers over your old sinful life so that His life is fully visible in your life.

Atonement means "a covering," and in the Old Testament the Mercy Seat covered the Ark of the Covenant. On the Day of Atonement, the High Priest sprinkled the blood of the sacrificial animal on the Mercy Seat as a covering for the sins of the people (Lev. 16:15-16). In the New Testament, Hebrews 9:11-12 states that Jesus became our eternal High Priest and accomplished our atonement once and for all time with His own blood. In your covenant with Jesus, your sinful past life is covered over and blotted out, leaving no record of it, and through His blood, you are justified before God. Indeed, in the words of the old hymn, there is "wonder-working power in His blood."

The covenant partners then shared a covenant meal in which they fed each other a piece of bread, symbolizing their body, and offered the other a sip of wine symbolizing their life. This is the origin of a bride and groom feeding each other a bite of wedding cake following their marriage ceremony.

This is also the basis of the Lord's Supper when Jesus took bread broke it and said, "This is My body which is given for you; do this in remembrance of Me." He also took the wine and said, "This cup is the new covenant in My blood, which is shed for you" (Luke 22:19-20). Sadly, many Christians have lost their understanding of the Lord's Supper. It is a covenant meal we share with Jesus in which we take His body and His life into our own life and become one with Him.

When two entered into a covenant, they lived exclusively for the other and found ultimate meaning and joy in their own life by bringing fulfillment to the life of the other. Their emotional, spiritual, and physical bond became so strong and binding until they shared each other's thoughts and actions and became one, even taking on a resemblance to the other. They became inseparable in a common life.

When you enter into the new covenant with Jesus, this is the nature of the Christian life He wants to share with you. He came to our earthly home and became like us so that He could take us to His heavenly home and enable us to be like Him. In that eternal, unbroken union, each of us becomes a part of the Bride of Christ.

Preparing a Place for the Bride

When Jesus said, "...I go to prepare a place for you...that where I am, there you may be also" (John 14:2-3), He was not only making a promise to His disciples—and to His Bride—but also fulfilling the ancient plan of God. Jesus didn't mean that He was going to prepare a new place from the ground up that hadn't previously existed, for that's not what the Bible states. Instead, He was making it ready. Literally, the image is to make everything ready and waiting when the opportunity arises for you to enter and dwell in this place. So, how long has the "place" Jesus prepared for His Bride existed? The answer is so amazing and mindboggling it defies comprehension. We can only think about it with awe and wonder.

Consider these Bible truths and allow them to sink deep into your spiritual understanding. In the beginning, God created a paradise setting for man known as the Garden of Eden. But there is a short phrase in the biblical description that powerfully reveals something deeper. The garden was "eastward in Eden," (Gen.1:8) and the word "east" is not limited in meaning to a location or direction. It also describes something that is first, or the first of a sequence—something that exists before anything else. Think of it this way: Everything that happens in a day is preceded by the sun rising in the east. So, before God created anything, He envisioned and planned a heavenly paradise for those who faithfully follow Him.

Later, God empowered Moses and Joshua to lead the Israelites to the Promised Land. It really should be thought of as the land where God would offer to fulfill every divine promise, if only His people would follow Him in faith. It was to be a land of peace and prosperity, "a land in which you will eat bread without scarcity, in which you will lack nothing" (Deut. 8:9), and a land so providentially abundant they could not consume one year's crops before the next overflow harvest was ready. It was a land of milk and honey (Jos. 5:6), and the word for "milk" describes a fat suckling calf so full of milk from nursing its mama that it can't hold any more.

This land was to be a physical glimpse of the spiritual kingdom of heaven awaiting God's faithful, covenant followers. But the blessings were delayed because the people refused to believe God's promises. They cheated themselves out of paradise.

In Proverbs 8:22-30, wisdom is described as if it were a person, and the writer states that wisdom (or the mind and divine purpose of God) was there "...at the beginning of His way...." After describing all that God created, the writer states, "When He marked out the foundations of the earth, then I was beside Him as a master craftsman, and I was daily in His delight." When John later wrote about the "Word" of God, it is this essence of God's expressed wisdom and God's nature, purpose, and plan that he is describing. The Greeks captured all these divine qualities in the word "logos."

Thus, John states, "In the beginning was the Word (logos), and the Word was with God, and the Word was God. He was in the beginning with God. All things were made through Him, and without Him nothing was made that was made" (John 1:1-3). Jesus is the incarnate Word of God and the incarnate wisdom of God. The Word (logos) became human flesh and lived among us (v.14). Prior to becoming man, the Word was there at the beginning of all creation, planning, working, and creating a paradise home for His Bride with the skill and devotion of "a master craftsman." Thus, it is as perfect and complete as God, in His infinite wisdom and power, can make it.

Everything that Jesus made since the beginning of time was done to reveal His love for His Bride and bring peace and joy into her life. Just like the "east of Eden," before anything else was created, the divine mind of God envisioned a place where Jesus would eternally live in a heavenly paradise with His Bride, the redeemed church, and that includes you and me.

One last thought: Consider the Parable of the Sheep and Goats (Matt.25:31-46). It is a parable cast in the everyday circumstance of a shepherd separating goats from his flock of sheep. Jesus used the parable to describe God's final judgment on the nations. The Son of Man will gather the sheep on His right hand and the goats on His left. Those on His left will be cast into everlasting damnation for their unfaithfulness. But, to those on His right hand, the King will say, "Come, you blessed of My Father, inherit the kingdom prepared for you from the foundation of the world" (v. 34).

Please realize that, if you are a Christian, you sit at the right hand of the King. The kingdom you will inherit as part of the Bride of Christ has been there for you since the beginning of time—before the foundation of the world was laid—from the east of Eden. Indeed, as the Bible states, "eye has not seen, nor ear heard, nor have entered into the heart of man the things which God has prepared for those who love Him" (1 Cor. 2:9). And He has prepared it all for the Bride of Christ.

The Helpmate

When God created Eve from Adam's rib, He permanently established a divine purpose for the Bride that has profound meaning today for Christians and for the church as a whole. God did not have to create Eve. Her existence is a divine act of grace. That same standard is true for us today. God did not have to save us, and God did not have to create the Bride, the redeemed church, but He did. Our eternal covenant life in Christ is a totally unmerited gift of divine love and grace. We should be overwhelmed with gratitude, thanksgiving, and praise for all that's been given to us, but, sadly, many Christians do not express that.

Adam was created in the image and likeness of God, and God breathed into Him "the breath of life; and man became a living being." The implication of this verse is that God breathed into Adam the eternal, sinless life of God. But that was not done for Eve. Even though the text states "male and female He created them," it does specifically state that Eve was created in God's image and likeness.

Eve, the Bride, was created much differently and for one purpose only. Eve's identity came from Adam, and so her life was to be a covenant reflection of him. Her life was to be "comparable" to Adam's, and thus she was to be like him in all her words and deeds.

What was true for Eve is true for Christians today and for the covenant Bride church as well. We have no life and no identity as Christians apart from Jesus.

Our eternal life is an extension of His eternal life.

The one thing that has deeply troubled and grieved me during my years of ministry is the failure of Christians to understand the meaning of the new birth. When you accept Jesus as savior, your old sinful life is crucified with Christ. But, through God's grace, you are raised from death in the power of Jesus' resurrection to a new, redeemed life. You are spiritually born again, and being born again in Christ is not the same as joining the church, getting baptized, and then sitting on the back pew.

This new life is not your own. It is Jesus' life given to you. Just like Eve's life was taken from Adam, your redeemed life was taken from Jesus, and it was given to you as a gift of love and grace based on your faith in Him.

Therefore, you are in a covenant with Jesus, and the purpose of your new life is to be a living expression of His life. You have become a "Christian," literally a Christ-like person. You have no life other than His life, just as Eve had no life other than Adam's. You are spiritually wed to Him as a part of His Bride, the redeemed, glorified church.

There is no room in your covenant life, or in the life of His Bride, for actions and attitudes other than those Jesus would have. If the Bible says, "apart from Me, you can do nothing" (John 15:5), you must grasp the truth that apart from Him, you are nothing. You have no life other than His. Very few Christians view themselves in this way.

Thus, in all of your actions and attitudes, you are to be a living reflection of Christ. Just as Eve was created to be "comparable" to Adam, you are to be comparable to Jesus in the way you live and love, and you are to be a physical expression of Jesus' spiritual nature implanted in you through your covenant with Him. You cannot openly profess to be a "new creature" in Christ in whom "the old things have passed away; behold, all things have become new" (2 Cor. 5:17) and then go back to your same old sinful prejudices, attitudes, and actions. The new blood covenant with Jesus does not work that way!

Because Eve had no life of her own other than what she received from Adam, her life was to have been an extension of his life, and thus she was created to be his "help-mate." That term is crucial in understanding our own Christian life. Just as Eve was divinely and graciously created for no other purpose than to be Adam's helper, so, too, is the Bride created to be Jesus' "helper," and that includes us. A deeper understanding of the role of the "help-mate" will transform your understanding your Christian responsibility to Jesus.

The Bride's Ministry

When God created Eve as Adam's "help-mate," He did not use one of Adam's toes so Eve could run errands for him. He did not use one of Adam's fingers so Eve could constantly use her hands cooking for him, washing his clothes, and trying to keep his house clean. God did not use other parts of Adam so Eve could have his children and stay up all night caring for a sick child while Adam slept.

Do I sound a bit cynical? Maybe, but that's the environment into which I was born. As a child, I was awakened numerous mornings by my parents fighting. My father used the Bible as his favorite arguing point: "You know what the Bible says. I'm the man of the house and you're my wife, and you'll do as I say and do whatever I tell you to do." The only problem was, she didn't.

My maternal grandmother bore thirteen children for my grandfather. Think about that a moment. During crushing poverty and family struggles, my grandpa kept my dear grandmother pregnant for nearly ten years, and he still expected her to cook three meals a day, milk the cows, tend the garden, wash clothes in a washpot over a fire in the yard, and iron all his clothes, including his underwear, with a heavy iron heated in front of a fire in the fireplace, even in July and August. A bit inconsiderate of him, don't you think? Did my grandfather love my grandmother or just use her? I've always had my own thoughts about it. So, let me emphatically state my opinion: That is NOT the kind of help-mate for Adam that God created Eve to be, and that is NOT the role of a wife in a covenant marriage.

The basic definition of Eve as Adam's help-mate means "a corresponding equal," or someone "comparable" to him. God could have used any part of Adam to create Eve, but He chose the part closest to Adam's heart—his rib. It was as if his heart and her heart were to beat with the same rhythm, and they were to be one in heart, mind, and soul, which is essentially the definition of a covenant marriage.

Although created from the dust of the earth, Adam's greatest characteristic was the divine Spirit of God within him, for he was created in God's spiritual image and likeness and possessed the "breath of life" divinely given to him. It is important to remember that Eve did not receive the breath of life, nor was she created in God's image, but she received those spiritual qualities as a gracious, free gift in her covenant relationship with Adam, just as we do in our relationship with Jesus.

Thus, as his "corresponding equal," Eve was to visibly reflect in her physical life all that Adam invisibly possessed in his spiritual life. That is the historic role of the biblical Bride, and it is the divine standard set for the Bride of Christ, the redeemed church, and for each of us as Christians.

The definition of Eve's role as Adam's help-mate yields an interesting example. The concept of a corresponding equal may also mean a "counter-weight." Most old elevators operated by using a counter-weight to offset the weight of the car. The weight of the elevator and the counter-weight were the same, and as the elevator went up, the adjacent counter-weight went down, and as the elevator went down, the weight went up, keeping it all in balance. Without the counter-weight, the elevator car would come crashing down.

Is there a spiritual lesson here? Yes. The spiritual essence of God's nature reaches its highest level when shared with another. Divine love, joy, peace, and all the other fruits of the Spirit (Gal.5: 22-23) must flow from one to another in a covenant—they cannot be kept inside. That was true for Adam and Eve, and it's true for Jesus and His Bride, the church.

When Eve fully received those divine spiritual qualities from Adam, she became physically comparable to what he was spiritually. As his counter-weight, she had the ability to either lift him up and help fulfill his godly purpose, or pull him down.

The Bride of Christ occupies the same role and responsibility. As Christians, we either lift up Christ in our physical life by revealing His spiritual nature within us, or we pull Him down by our sinful attitudes and actions that are totally unlike Him, while proclaiming to be a Christian.

The church, and we as individual Christians, are called out of our attraction to this world and set apart and sanctified as the only people on this earth commissioned to be living witnesses for Christ and the truth of the gospel. We receive His spiritual nature into our physical life through repentance and a new birth, making us a new person in Jesus.

Through the power of the Holy Spirit, the divine work of this new life is to love God with all our heart and our neighbor as our self—without condition, prejudice, or judgmental condemnation of others. We become the light of the world, and we glorify Jesus in the world by revealing in our physical life the same qualities He possesses in His spiritual life. We are to be comparable to Him, and when we are, we become true Christians— sincere, faithful, Christ-like servants who bear much fruit for Him.

Maybe you've never thought of yourself as Jesus' help-mate, but you are. Not only does the heavenly kingdom you will inherit go back to the beginning of time, but the purpose of your life as a Christian help-mate goes back to the very first bride, Eve.

The Unfaithful Bride

Something went wrong in the Garden of Eden, terribly wrong. We can blame the satanic serpent, the forbidden fruit, or the disobedience of Adam and Eve, but the dominant nature of God was replaced by the dominating nature of human sin, and mankind is still suffering the consequences.

So, what happened? More importantly, if this spiritual disaster happened to Adam and Eve, can the same downfall happen to us today as individual Christians and to the church, the Bride of Christ? The answer is quite sobering.

It began with Eve and spread to Adam. Eve was created comparable to Adam, and her only purpose was to reflect physically what he was spiritually, and thus bring fulfillment to his godly purpose, just as we are to glorify Christ. She was in covenant with him, and his life was her life. The divine life as Adam's covenant bride should have brought Eve unlimited joy and happiness, just as being in the new covenant with Jesus should bring us consummate joy in life.

But, it didn't. She wanted more, even as many Christians do. Eve was the first to lose the battle of spiritual faith versus physical feelings. Rather than believing "the just shall live by faith," Eve accepted the satanic lie that the role of the Bride was best experienced through human emotions of pride, pleasure, and power. She rejected the idea that sin had consequences, and instead decided she could satisfy her physical desires while also proclaiming herself as Adam's bride.

And so the Bride became worldly, and she continues to be. The fundamental purpose of the church—to be the covenant Bride of Christ and serve Him only as His living witness by going into every corner of the world sharing the gospel—has given way to the compromised Bride. Though countless local congregations still faithfully serve, there are many reasons to be concerned for the Christian church.

Today, the Bride of Christ in America far too often glorifies mega-churches with millionaire pastors who preach self-enrichment, but never call for repentance and turning from sin. She builds lavish temples of worship that testify to her riches, but neglects to feed the poor and care for the least among us. She has leaders who fawn over politicians and political power without demanding justice for the poor and needy from those unprincipled leaders who they idolize. She has turned worship into entertainment with silly preachers standing in God's pulpit dressed as if they were going to a cookout and telling meaningless stories instead of powerfully preaching the word of God through the inspiration of the Holy Spirit.

When the church stopped preaching and praying and started swinging and swaying in worship, she stopped being the Bride. She leads millions astray by repeating the devil's lie, "Has God really said you can't do that?" She spreads the sinful idea that human sin doesn't have divine consequences, and that the role of the Bride of Christ is best experienced through human feelings rather than fidelity to Jesus. Sadly, millions of so-called Christians believe this is what church is all about.

Is there an answer? Yes, but few Christians have read it, much less believe it. Revelation 2:4-5, which is Jesus' message to the church at Ephesus, states, "...you have left your first love. Remember therefore from where you have fallen; repent and do the first works...." When the Bride of Christ returns to her first love for Jesus and the gospel, faithfully shares this glorious truth to all people without compromise or prejudice, and in all her words and deeds again becomes "comparable" to Jesus, we will have an unprecedented spiritual awakening in America.

Maybe that is why the Bible concludes with both the Spirit and the Bride crying out to Jesus, "Come!" May God have mercy on us and again make the church the true covenant Bride of Christ!

Whose Side is God On?

An evangelical political strategist recently boasted, "We have God on our side." It reminded me of perhaps the most amazing preaching experience in my ministry career.

I was serving as an interim pastor in a rural community, and the National Guard units from two nearby towns had been mobilized for deployment to Iraq in the first Gulf War. Several families in the church were impacted and understandably upset.

I had prepared a sermon for the Sunday morning service, but just didn't feel right about it—something was missing. As the choir sang their special prior to the sermon, I was simply scanning through my Bible, and I noticed the passage where Joshua was about to lead his army against enemy forces occupying the Promised Land. He saw an unusual figure, who he considered to be a Man of God, and Joshua asked him, "Are You for us or our adversary?"

It was like a bolt of divine lightning struck. There was an immediate, overwhelming conviction, as if the voice of God was speaking to me that said, "Here is your sermon. Now stand up and preach it!" The choir was concluding the special music, and I knew I had no choice but to trust and obey.

I explained to the congregation what had happened and told them that whatever the sermon turned out to be, it was from the Holy Spirit and not me. It was an amazing and powerful twenty minutes that left us all in tears.

Here were two armies about to do battle, and both claimed to worship the same God, only very differently. So, whose side was God on? Could we ask Him the same question: "Are you for us or our adversary?"

Here's what God spoke to us that morning:

God is on the side of those who fight for what is right in His sight, not in the eyes of man.

Politics is not the same as the righteousness of God, and you make a great error trying to enlist God in your army. We are to put on the armor of God and fight for what is right to Him, not what seems right and politically correct to us. We are to put on the breastplate of His righteousness, not try to hang a flag around the shoulders of Almighty God.

We are to fight for divine truth that glorifies God everywhere in the world, not just a military or political cause that glorifies us. We are to fight for justice and freedom for all, both in other lands when needed, and here in America also.

We are to fight for the liberation of the soul and the human spirit so that those burdened down with fear, inequality, and hopelessness can know what liberty and justice for all really means, whether in Iraq, the United States, or right here in Mississippi.

We must never confuse God's plan of redemption for all mankind through faith in Christ with a political agenda or the glory and ego of any human leader. We must fight for truth, righteousness, integrity, honesty, humility, true concern for all people, whether rich or poor, so that we truly are one nation under God.

When we do that, whether in some foreign land or here in America, we discover the answer to the question: "Are You for us or our adversary?"

As long as American citizens are willing to put on the armor of God and fight for what is right in God's sight, He will lead us to victory.

Does God Make Ugly

When the Physical Fails You

The older I get, the uglier I become. Maybe I should be kind to myself and say the more "unhandsome" I become. Yeah, yeah, my English minor tells me that's not a word, but it gets my point across. Change in one's appearance is just part of life's aging process, and there's not much one can do.

I could get one of those nip and tuck operations and remove the wrinkles from under my chin, but if they pulled all that skin tight, my belly button would be in the middle of my chest. I'm not so ugly yet that I have to hang a pork chop around my neck so my dogs will play with me, but sometimes I don't turn the light on when I brush my teeth. I can almost scare my own self.

Not long ago, I was socializing with my three pet turkeys, Moe, Larry, and Curly, and the issue of ugly came up. It wasn't a deep conversation—we were just talking turkey—but I told them how ugly they were. They all three gobbled in return, seemingly in agreement. Although, they could have been asking me if I had looked in a mirror recently. Anyway, no one was offended, and we remained friends, but they're still ugly by human standards.

Have you ever looked closely at a turkey's head? It looks like God made them last and used whatever paint and parts he had left over from making other creatures and hung it around a big bird's body and said, "Behold, the turkey." Then He gave them a voice that sounds like a thirty-year-old pickup that barely runs, and it slams on brakes and falls apart in your driveway, complete with screeching, banging, and clanging so weird that people actually have contests to see if they can duplicate the sound. Seriously, have you ever heard of a redbird calling contest?

I really pondered this question: Does God make ugly? Does God look down on Moe, Larry, and Curley and say to Himself, "I can't believe I made something so ugly!" Does He sometime say the same about me? No, I don't think that word is in His vocabulary. It's a man-made concept.

Did you know that God used some of the oldest and probably "ugliest" people to do some of His greatest work? By looking at a couple of examples, it might help all of us in the so-called "over the hill" club to find a new level of joy and contentment about ourselves. If we can, it would be a lot more comforting than a new pair of flannel pj's from Wal-Mart.

An Old Priest Without a Voice

Zacharias was an elderly priest who still faithfully performed his Temple duties. The priests and Levites drew lots to determine various priestly functions, and Zacharias drew the responsibility of burning incense. As the smoke drifted upward, it symbolized the prayers of the people going up to God, including Zacharias' personal prayers. It was a solemn, holy responsibility.

Zacharias' wife was Elizabeth, who was also from a family of priests, and together they had faithfully served God for many years. But sadly, their greatest prayer had never been answered, for they were now elderly and childless.

While burning the incense, an angel appeared to Zacharias and told him his prayer had been heard and Elizabeth would bear him a son, whose name would be John. Zacharias was confused and gripped in fear. "How is this possible?" he asked the angel. "I'm old and so is my wife." The vision was so mindboggling that Zacharias simply could not believe what he had seen and heard. Strangely, because of his unbelief, the angel made Zacharias mute until the baby was born. But, indeed these two old people experienced a miracle of joy they never dreamed possible.

The baby's birth was a time of great celebration, and many wondered if he would be named Zacharias, after his father. The old priest, still unable to speak, wrote on a piece of paper, "No, his name is John." Immediately, he was able to speak again, and the people around marveled. The name John basically means, "God has been gracious, has shown favor." It was the perfect name for the future ministry of this child.

Many people fail to understand the ministry of John the Baptist. He did far more than baptize Jesus. There was a historic belief the prophet Elijah would reappear prior to the arrival of the long-awaited messiah and personally declare the messiah's identity. The angel specifically said that John "would go before Him in the spirit and power of Elijah...and make ready a people prepared for the Lord."

Indeed, John's powerful preaching drew multitudes of people into the Judean wilderness who responded to John's call for spiritual change through repentance. Can you imagine the drama? If John was the spirit of Elijah, then the messiah was about to appear and dramatically change life as they knew it. John not only prepared the heart of the people for Jesus' preaching, but he also specifically identified Him as the Messiah of God when he declared, "Behold the Lamb of God who takes away the sin of the world."

When Zacharias started speaking again, he described the ministry his son would have. Can you imagine the joy he and Elizabeth experienced knowing how amazingly God had answered their prayers. What an awesome blessing for these two old people to know their son would prepare the way for others to hear the gospel of Jesus!

Please believe me when I tell you this: You are never too old, never too feeble, never too worn out, and never too unappealing and unattractive for God to use you in a powerful way to change someone else's life for good. When you do, divine joy will fill your life, just as it did for Zacharias and Elizabeth.

Joseph's Choice

Joseph was likely an older man, probably not all that physically appealing any longer. He is not mentioned again after Jesus' twelfth birthday, and James, the brother of Jesus, described pure religion as visiting widows and orphans and helping with their needs. Was this a glimpse of Jesus' childhood years? Was Mary the last chance for Joseph to find happiness?

Whatever the answers might have been, Joseph was now shocked, angry, and humiliated. Mary, the young woman to whom he was engaged, had devastated him. As part of the marriage preparation, the religious law of Israel required that she be examined physically to ensure she was still a virgin. It was a degrading and embarrassing procedure, but required by law to root out harlotry and keep Israel pure. To Joseph's utter dismay, Mary was pregnant. Now he was faced with the legally required punishment. He and other men of the community were required to stone Mary to death at her father's front door. It would be a brutal, horrendous execution of the woman he planned to marry, but he had no choice under the demands of the religious law.

Then, Mary offered the preposterous excuse that God had caused her to get pregnant, and she had not been with a man. Was she crazy? Did she really think he would believe her? The pressure on Joseph mounted as community religious zealots vocally demanded that Mary be killed. She was nothing but a cheap, adulterous harlot, and God would be pleased for Israel to be rid of trash like her and the influence she would have on others. The best way to rid the country of sin was to kill the sinners, they insisted.

But Joseph resisted their demands and instead said that he would deal with Mary privately. These blood-thirsty religious purists would be denied the savage pleasure of casting stones at Mary and beating her on her head with rocks until she was a lifeless, bloody sinner on whom they had unleashed divine justice. Joseph would do it himself.

And then the angel of God told him it was true: Mary was indeed with Child by the Spirit of God, and the Child she would bear would be the Messiah of God. This Child would fulfill the prophet Isaiah's cherished prediction that a virgin would conceive and bear a Son, and His name would be "Immanuel," meaning "God with us." This faithful, caring young woman had found favor with God, and she would be the mother of His only begotten Son.

Joseph struggled spiritually with the contradiction between the law and God's love for Mary. She was now considered to be a sinful harlot who had lost her virginity—a filthy blot on Israel's religious purity—and everything Joseph had been taught about God and religion demanded that Mary should be killed.

Yet, now he believed that God had chosen Mary to be His chosen vessel through whom the savior of the world would be born. One of the greatest Christian miracles was when Joseph decided he would be guided by love and not by law. We have him to thank for Jesus being born.

If you want to experience the meaning of the birth of Jesus, commit yourself to God's redeeming love revealed through Him. Stop judging others when you have no idea how God is working in their life. Share in the amazement of how God can use someone as His chosen vessel to reveal Himself that religious zealots have condemned. Embrace the unloved, the sinners around you, and the lost and lonely. Put down your stones and stop thinking you are good enough to cast them at another when the burden of sin on your shoulders keeps you from even raising your arms. Marvel at God's amazing love and grace when He took a scared yet faithful young woman, who everyone considered to be a cheap whore worthy of death, and made her the mother of our Savior.

It doesn't matter what others think of you, just as it didn't matter what others thought of Mary. Will it change your life? Just ask Joseph.

He Laughed

They were a delightful old couple, somewhat advanced in age. He was ninety-nine and she was a bit younger at ninety. But despite all their efforts and prayers over the years, they were childless, and the sadness they felt left them both questioning life and even God. Now, they were both so elderly neither gave any thought to family, and both were sadly reconciled to the loneliness of old age.

The old man was good and godly, as faithful to God as he could be, and, strangely, he began having this mysterious and indescribable feeling that he was yet going to be a father. He dismissed it at first as a silly idea, but the thought persisted and became so strong it was as if the voice of God was speaking and assuring him it was true. He wanted to believe; but physical facts assailed his faith. "It's just not possible," he thought to himself, especially at my age. And what about my wife? She never had a child in her younger years, and she sure can't conceive in her nineties. The whole idea was so laughable, even preposterous, that he fell face down on the ground in laughter? But the thought persisted and wouldn't leave him.

Sometime later, he was sitting near the door of his dwelling, trying to find coolness in the heat of the day, when the Lord personally appeared to him and assured him that the promised birth of a child was true. The old gentleman didn't realize it, but his wife was standing behind him and overheard him talking to God about the promised birth of a baby. She, like her husband, also started laughing at the absurdity of the idea. She had never laughed so hard in ninety years, and she couldn't stop, as the tears of laughter ran down her cheeks.

"Look at me," she blurted out to her husband. "You seriously think a wrinkled, broke down, ugly old woman like me can have a baby? And even if I could, what's it going to nurse nurse on? Have you noticed these two old flabby goat skins lately that hang down nearly to my waist? Poor thing would starve to death in a week." She laughed some more.

"And you ain't no spring rooster yourself. You can crow about this all you want to—and I don't want to hurt your feelings—but some parts of you haven't worked in years, if you know what I mean." She burst out laughing again.

But he persisted in his belief, and she finally gave in to his crazy idea. Astonishingly, in response to his faith a miracle happened, and they were able to share the pleasures of marriage neither had known for years. And that miracle was followed by another miracle: She discovered she was pregnant. Both of them laughed at the amazing, mind-boggling joyous reality of it all.

In due time, she gave birth to a baby boy. But her pain of childbirth gave way to the joy of motherhood after all those empty years—and she laughed, and all her family and friends laughed with her. "Who would have ever thought that an old ninety-year-old woman would be nursing her new-born son?" she said in amazement. Now her laughter was no longer the laughter of disbelief, but rather the joyous, unrestrained laughter only a miracle can produce—the laughter of an unimaginable life she never dreamed would be possible.

His name was Abraham and her name was Sarah. Abraham named the baby Isaac, which means "laughter, or he laughed." Years later, Isaac would become the father of Jacob, and his sons would become the founding leaders of the twelve tribes of Israel.

God used these two old, withered-up people, both bearing the worn out, unappealing signs of age, to establish the Jewish faith and later the nation of Israel through their descendants. From that, Christianity emerged, and its religious and cultural values produced Western Civilization as we know it today. When those values of faith and freedom were brought to this land, the United States of America was born. You and I are who we are today as a nation, as a culture, and as individuals because of these two old people laughing in joyous amazement at the miracle of life God graciously gave them.

It doesn't matter how old you are, how puny you may feel, or what you look like. If you can discover a similar joy in celebrating the birth of Jesus, you, too, can experience divine joy in a way that you may have been longing for all your life.

Go ahead, laugh if you don't believe me, but it's true.

A Baptist Boy Goes to Mass

When I went to Mass for the first time, it wasn't the proverbial "bull in a China shop" where something gets broken with every twist and turn, but it wasn't far from it. My uncle and aunt lived in Hattiesburg, were devout Catholics, and attended Sacred Heart Catholic Church.

I, on the other hand, was an inquisitive country kid who attended the old wood-framed Good Hope Baptist Church two miles west of Purvis. The difference between the two churches was like night and day.

I was visiting my aunt and cousins, and being faithful to their beliefs, they attended Mass and took me with them. What an eye-opening experience that was, and what an embarrassment I was.

First, for any of my Catholic friends, please take no offense at this, but try to experience my first visit to a Catholic church from my little Baptist country boy perspective, and, hopefully, you will find it amusing.

The first thing that got my curiosity was the bowl of water just inside the door. One of my cousins whispered that it was Holy Water, but that didn't clarify much. Everyone stopped and dipped their fingers in the water and then touched their forehead and chest, and I couldn't understand why. The only thing I was accustomed to at Good Hope was the men stopping at the front door and taking one last big drag off their Camel cigarette before going inside. Apparently, a good shot of nicotine got them closer to Jesus, but I had never seen anyone dip their fingers in water when they entered the church house.

Once I got past the Holy Water, I looked around in awe. Never had I seen this many candles in one room, along with all the statues. I know my little mouth hung open in amazement. That's when embarrassment number one happened.

I was slowly walking along behind my aunt and cousins, staring in amazement and not watching what was happening in front of me. No one told me they would kneel in the aisle before entering the pew area. So, while counting candles, I didn't see them kneel, and I tripped over them. I was so embarrassed, but I still didn't know whether I was supposed to kneel or remain standing. I didn't kneel, and I could have sworn there were glances in my direction wondering who that little heathen was.

Then, instead of sitting down in the pew and turning through a Heavenly Highway Hymnal looking for a song to request, like everyone did at Good Hope, my aunt and cousins knelt down on this little board anchored to the pew in front of us and started praying. Nobody did that at Good Hope. I was used to only one person praying at a time, and it was usually an older member who knew everybody's sins and could sack them up and get them before the Lord for forgiveness.

I always wondered what all was included in "our many sins and shortcomings" for which forgiveness was sought on a weekly basis, but I knew there must have been some interesting stories buried in there. Maybe that's why some of the men yelled "Amen" so loudly at the end of the prayer, apparently believing their sin slate had been wiped clean and they could start over again. So, was I to pray or not pray? I didn't pray; I was still trying to get a good count on the candles.

When the Mass concluded, we exited by passing in front of the altar. I had never seen such a beautiful display in a church. Once again, no one told me they would kneel when passing the altar, and with my one good eye on the statue of Mary, I tripped like I did the first time. Luckily, I didn't fall or make someone yell in pain.

I simply had never seen anything like that. All we had at Good Hope was an offering table in front of the pulpit with two empty offering plates on it and occasionally some flowers. I think the table might have been an economy model, because I don't recall "In Remembrance" being carved on the front. Well, I left the church without messing up anymore, or breaking anything, but I wondered about the service for a long time. You have to understand the religious influence in my young life. Because of my parents' divorce, my conservative, opinionated, unyielding grandfather was my father figure, and he spoke harshly of any belief other than his own. He wasn't fond of the Pope, considered anyone who spoke in tongues and practiced faith healing to be "holy rollers," and slammed the idea of baptism by sprinkling. According to him, you needed to be totally dunked in flowing water, not in some built-in baptistry, for baptism to be real. That is what I was taught as a child, and it greatly influenced my early religious beliefs.

But I privately struggled with whether everyone else was wrong. How could anyone be so faithful, prayerful, and devoted to God and still be wrong?

How could those who professed to be the only ones who were right be so cold and judgmental while those who were supposed to be wrong could be so caring, compassionate, and embody the essence of Christian faith, as I understood it. There were times when it was so confusing to me.

Then one day I found this verse in my Bible, and I have pondered its meaning in relation to diverse religious practices ever since: "...if you confess with your mouth the Lord Jesus and believe in your heart that God has raised Him from the dead, you will be saved." That's it; nothing else. From the birth of Christianity, man has tried to add something else to faith. The Greeks said it was faith in Jesus plus human knowledge; early Jewish believers argued that it was faith plus Jewish ritual; others said there must be faith plus a separate infusion of Holy Spirit power and speaking in tongues.

The great tragedy of Christianity is that we left the simplicity of the message and for 2000 years have fought over the mechanics of worship, often brutally. Christianity has a sad history of intolerance of other views, and I once was guilty myself.

Maybe I'm just mellowing in my old age. But when you peel back all the superfluous leaves of denominational beliefs and practices and find the fruit of the Spirit, here it is—if you truly confess your personal faith in Jesus as Lord in your life and you believe that God raised Him from the dead, you will be saved. All the rest are add-ons. If you don't believe me, read Romans 10:9. Those are the words of the Apostle Paul, who wrote about two-thirds of the New Testament. He should know.

The passage of time has a unique way of softening one's view of things. The words of "September Song" seem to capture my spiritual metamorphosis: "Oh, it's a long, long while from May to December, but the days get short when you reach September...the days dwindle down to a precious few...September, November..." Back in life's springtime days of May, I could be vocally dogmatic about Baptist doctrine. But my November days are upon me, and the days are getting shorter. Others can now argue over the Baptist Faith and Message, or whatever denominational creed or statement they may follow. For me, none of that is really controlling any more. Its significance has faded in my life like the autumn leaves that have fallen.

In my quiet moments of meditation and prayer, I just go back to the simple promise of God's word. I openly profess my faith in Jesus as my Lord and

Savior, and I truly believe God raised Him from the dead. Therefore, I am saved, and I am eternally secure in Christ. Whatever the December days of my life my hold, I have no fear. I am at peace with God.

You can be, too, whether you are Baptist, Methodist, Presbyterian, Episcopalian, Catholic, or any other. Stop fussing and fighting over the mechanics of your religion and instead focus on the message of Jesus. It's repentance and faith in Jesus—just faith.

My Greatest Ministry Disappointment

If I am guilty of one thing, it is that I believe Christian action is more important than religious words. If we aren't willing to forgive, then don't preach about it. If we aren't willing to put personal, petty differences aside for the glory of Christ and the building up of His Church, then stifle all the meaningless blabber about being reconciled to one another. If you can't truly live it, then why bother to proclaim it?

I have never heard of two churches, which had split apart, coming back together in love, forgiveness, and mutually reconciling themselves as one through the power of the Holy Spirit. What an amazing Christian testimony and witness that would be, and what enormous opportunity for Christian growth would be experienced by all.

I began to actively work toward accomplishing this goal, and the pastor of Coaltown (not the present pastor) and I met several times for prayer and discussion about how it could happen. I'll have to admit, I thought a miracle of Christian love was occurring.

But I guess I was too much of a dreamer, and I didn't understand human emotion well enough. My dream was short lived. Before long, the gossip started, misrepresentations abounded, I was told I was crazy for such an idea, and one older gentleman personally asked me, "Preacher, did you kind of lose your mind there for a little while?"

And, so the dream died. The churches remained separated, reconciliation never happened, and we had no more joint services. Today, both churches seem to be doing well, and that's good. But, about thirty years ago, the members of both missed the greatest opportunity to demonstrate to all in this community what Christian love, forgiveness, and reconciliation is all about, and that is sad to me.

It devastated me both personally and spiritually. Not only were the personal comments hurtful, but the sense of failure I experienced was heartbreaking. I could not get my own family, friends, neighbors, and church members to see the truth of Christ's love for us, and how we are then to love one another. In 1990, I resigned as pastor at Good Hope and moved on.

I have always felt that I failed in the greatest opportunity of Christian leadership I was given. That failure is my greatest ministry disappointment.

Sitting on a Ledge

It began uneventfully as a seminary class field trip to a New Orleans hospital, but it ended in a dramatic life-altering experience. As I exited the medical center, a crowd of people had gathered looking upward, and some were pointing to a man sitting on the eighth-floor ledge of a nearby multi- story parking garage with his legs dangling over the side. "He's gonna jump!" someone loudly exclaimed.

No sooner than I saw him, a policeman hurriedly walked past headed toward the garage. Without thinking of the possible consequences, I told the policeman I was a minister, if I could be of any help. Apparently, my credentials didn't overly impress him, because without hardly slowing down, he said, "What the heck, who knows what he might want, come on."

I rode with the officer to the eighth floor where other policemen were gathered outside the elevator. One of them commented, "All he wants is a priest." My NOPD escort with the bubbly personality replied, "I got one right here." At that moment my heart skipped a beat, my knees got wobbly, and I wanted to slam it in reverse for a reason most of you aren't aware of: I am deathly afraid of heights. I'm not just talking about flying at 30, 000 feet; I'm talking about the top of a step ladder height. In painting the nine- foot-high walls in this old house I'm renovating, I can go up about three steps on my ladder and that's my limit. I don't know how many of you have ever churned buttermilk by hand the old-fashioned way, but I shake so badly I could tie a gallon of clabber to my ladder and I'd have buttermilk when I got down.

So, the policemen at the elevator told me to go talk to the guy and see what I could do. They were so nonchalant about the situation, it's a wonder they didn't order pizza and beer while they watched me.

Nervously, I walked slowly toward the man. Like some movie scene, he told me to stop midway and turn completely around so he could see my back— and not to get close to him. There was about a four-foot-high retaining wall at the edge with roughly an eighteen-inch ledge on the outside of the wall. That's where he was sitting, and he could barely see over the top of the wall to talk to me.

I walked to the retaining wall approximately fifteen feet from him and told him who I was. Then I made a terrible mistake: I looked down. Just eight floors of the smell of New Orleans between me and the sidewalk. I froze in fear!

Looking down, I could see a crowd of miniature people standing beside their little toy cars staring up at the man and me. I really thought I was going to faint. But then the guy began talking to me. Maybe he thought he was going to have to rescue me instead of me rescuing him.

He began telling me what a mess he was in—family problems, unemployed, health issues—a whole litany of burdens that had become seemingly unbearable. But, here's how God can miraculously put you in the right spot at the right time to help another hurting person. He was a truck driver. My brother was also in the trucking business, and a little trucking knowledge had rubbed off on me. So, I asked him what make of truck he liked, and we had an in-depth discussion about the merits of Peterbilt, Kenworth, and other kinds of trucks eight floors up watching pigeons fly past. That's when he began to trust me.

I had gradually eased closer to him, without his objection, until I was almost beside him—he was still on the ledge and I was leaning over the retaining wall. I promised him if he would come to the seminary the next morning, I would find someone who could help him. I assured him there were people who cared about him, and that his life was not hopeless. He silently looked into my face, as if he were daring himself to believe me.

And then God did a miracle. I took one last step toward him, leaned as far out over the retaining wall as I could, and extended my hand to him. For that fateful moment, with me looking at him and at the concrete sidewalk eight floors below, the fear of heights left me.

He stared at me for several seconds and then slowly reached for my outstretched hand, which he solidly gripped. The ledge was so narrow I basically had to pull him up to where he could get his feet under him and stand. One slip and we both would have fallen to our deaths.

I helped him over the retaining wall, and he, a few of the policemen, and I went back to the ground floor. I gave him my name and telephone number and told him to please contact me if I could help him.

Throughout the whole ordeal I kept telling him that Jesus loved him, and the Lord not only knew every problem he faced, but He also had an answer for every need he had. I assured him that through faith in Christ, he could overcome his worst fear and still have a meaningful, productive life.

He never contacted me, and I don't know what happened to him. But, the more I thought about the words of assurance I spoke to him, the more I realized how they had applied to me also. God helped me overcome my worst fear in that pivotal moment to save the life of another hurting soul.

He can do the same for you. It may not be as dramatic as hanging from an eighth-floor ledge preventing a suicide, but Jesus can cast aside your greatest fear and uncertainty and give you strength and courage to help lift another hurting person from the pit of despair and hopelessness. So, if the need ever arises, don't be afraid to go out on a ledge to help someone.

Who Was That Visitor in Sunday School?

I was blessed with the opportunity to teach a unique Sunday School class at First Baptist Church in Jackson before becoming a pastor. Composed mainly of young professionals who wanted the freedom to explore topics outside of the standard quarterly material, the class was part of the "early church" Sunday School structure. As a recent seminary graduate, I was invited to be the teacher. It was an honor, but the responsibility was challenging. There was always lively discussion about the topics we studied and many thoughtful, probing questions.

But, one Sunday our class had an unexpected and unforgettable visitor. Shortly after we began, the door slowly opened and a young man quietly entered and took a seat along the aisle about midway of the class. Standing at the front, I immediately saw him, and I was shocked and surprised by his appearance.

He was around thirty years of age, with long brown hair, a trimmed beard, and wearing a white robe that went down below his knees. The robe was a coarse-looking material, slightly stained in a few places, but otherwise clean. His sandals were worn and well-traveled.

Some class members seemed a bit uneasy by his presence. I could tell from their facial expressions that most assumed he was a stoned-out character who was likely to cause disruption by sharing some bizarre, unappealing religious philosophy. On the contrary, he was polite and quiet.

I welcomed him and asked if he lived in Jackson. "No," he softly replied. Looking around the class, he said, "I was working like all of you. But I felt a deeper calling and began traveling around the country to different cities and towns telling people about God and about my faith in Him. I just rely on Him to provide my needs each day as I travel and share the gospel." What he said silenced me, sent a few goose bumps up my spine, and left me wondering who he really was.

He made no further comments, and quietly listened to our lesson. However, he frequently looked around the room at each person he could see, as if he were intently looking not into their face but rather into their soul. It wasn't a rude, impolite stare, but more like the deep, compassionate gaze of a father looking into the eyes of his questioning child or a loving teacher looking into the face of an amazed student experiencing the wonder of a new truth. Describing the emotional reaction he caused is challenging, but I had this deep, eerily spiritual feeling that I was in the presence of an extraordinary person.

When the class ended, I wanted to immediately go to him and ask more questions, but I was slightly delayed by a couple of students making comments to me about the lesson material. However, as I watched him leave the room, while answering the questions, I sadly noted that no one shook his hand or talked to him.

When I was free, after only two or three minutes, I could not find him. I looked down the surrounding halls, other adjacent classrooms, the church sanctuary, and even the restrooms. I went outside and walked completely around the church and checked the nearby parking areas. I never saw him again. A young man wearing a white robe amidst all of the well-dressed worshippers had completely disappeared from sight.

By now, my heart was slightly pounding, and I was filled with an unusual, uncertain emotion. Who was he? Where was he from and where did he go? How does someone in a white robe just disappear from view on a beautiful Sunday morning? I confess, I was totally perplexed by both his appearance and the quiet, unassuming manner of his visitation. I have never forgotten him.

Hebrews 13:3 states, "Do not forget to entertain strangers, for by so doing some have unwittingly entertained angels." Is that who he was...an angel? Or, more realistically, was he simply an eccentric wanderer off the street with some kind of warped messianic complex?

But, the more I wondered about him, his message, and his appearance, the more I was spiritually compelled to ask myself this: Was He Jesus who just wanted to visit our class and see for Himself how serious we were about serving and worshiping Him? That may sound a little bizarre, but there's nothing in the Bible that says Jesus couldn't do that if he chose to. It surely wouldn't be His Second Coming, but more like a brief visit to personally watch and listen to those who proclaimed faith in Him and professed to be His living witnesses.

If he had walked into your Sunday School class, what would have been your reaction? If he had entered your church worship service, would he have been welcomed? Would you have sat beside him?

It's been many years since he appeared, but I still ask myself this simple question that I've never been able to satisfactorily answer: "Who was he?"

Just Put Your Hand on the Radio

My left eye was severely injured in a home accident when I was two years old, and I permanently lost most of my sight in that eye. Even today, vision in my left eye is like looking through a fogged-up window.

Then, when I was in college, I was diagnosed with a deterioration of the retina in my right eye, and I was told by ophthalmologists that I would be blind within ten years. I attended law school with financial assistance from Mississippi Vocational Rehabilitation, Division of the Blind. It was that serious.

I had the first of two cornea transplants when I was fifteen (the second was ten years later), so you can imagine how worried I was as a young teenager about my eye condition. But I found hope on the radio.

I started listening to various radio preachers, and Billy Graham was my favorite. I even listened to Herbert W. Armstrong and his son, Garner Ted Armstrong, telling me about "The World Tomorrow" on the Radio Church of God. But, the one I pinned my hopes on was Oral Roberts, because he emphatically promised me that "something good is going to happen to you today!" In my case, something good would mean either getting my vision restored or escaping the dairy farm. Oral Roberts was very convincing; I actually believed him.

The best way I could hear Brother Oral was sitting in the old '61 Chevrolet at night in the middle of the backyard, constantly adjusting the radio dial to compensate for the come-and-go reception. Oral Roberts not only preached to me about Jesus and repentance (and as many bad things as I said about the dairy farm and Holstein cows, Lord knows I needed repentance), but he also told me the one thing I desperately wanted to hear—I could be healed! My left eye could have perfect vision again. All I had to do was put my hand on the radio while he preached, believe in faith, and expect a miracle. Brother Oral said it would happen, and I believed him—for a while.

So, here I sat in the car with the windows down on a hot, muggy Mississippi night, getting eaten up by mosquitoes, and with the volume cranked up as loud as possible so I wouldn't miss a word of his prophetic instructions. It was so loud the dogs started barking.

When he asked if anyone was sick or had a dreaded disease, I wanted to shout with faithful anticipation, "I do, Brother Oral, I do." He assured me Jesus could see me, even hunkered down in the Chevy Impala.

Then came his thundering instruction, "Put your hand on the radio and BELIEVE!" I wasn't sure if I was getting the full dose, because the car radio was in the dash, and I didn't know which would be better—put my hand on top of the dashboard above the radio, or push my hand against the front of the radio, hopefully without hitting a button and changing stations. For goodness' sake, I didn't want to lose Oral in the middle of a miracle and have to listen to Chicago White Sox baseball instead.

So, following this man of God's instructions—at least that's what the announcer said about him—I put my hand on the radio, closed my eyes, wrinkled up my face trying to conjure up all the faith I could, and put all my hopes in Oral Robert's promises. Guess what?

When I nervously opened my eyes, I was still just as blind in my left eye as before, but Oral was still telling me to put my hand on the radio and "Be Healed!" I tried again, and still nothing happened. I wanted to yell, "What am I doing wrong, Brother Oral?" I had my hand on the radio, I was believing as hard as I could, but the "something good" Oral had promised would happen to me today didn't happen. I was still blind in one eye and still milking cows. There was no miracle in the ole Chevy that night—just a lot of mosquitoes. There was a fly in the buttermilk somehow.

Then I got really worried that it was me—that my fifteen-year-old faith wasn't enough to please God. But, how does a country kid drum up enough faith for an Oral Roberts healing? It really bothered me. A few nights later, I tried again...same procedure...hand on the radio...eyes closed...head shaking trying to prove to Oral and God that I really did believe...slowly opening my eyes hoping for the miracle Oral promised...still blind.

But I refused to give up. If Oral Roberts promised it, surely it would happen. Maybe the radio wasn't working right, or there was too much static. Maybe the barking dogs were messing up the transmission of my promised healing. I tried several more times on other nights, even pulling out the car antenna as high as it would go so I could get the miracle Oral Roberts was sending to me in the old Chevy. Same result...still blind. Finally, in despair and frustration, I gave up. I can still remember the pain of feeling like a failure.

I have to confess that I was a slow learner when it came to radio and television faith healers. At first, I naively trusted them to be doing God's work with a pure heart and honest motives. Then, I began seeing some of it for what it is, even with my one good eye. If these preachers were divinely blessed by God with a gift of healing that would eliminate suffering, why did they want money to share that gift? Jesus never asked for a contribution to heal the sick. Why did Oral Roberts need to build a hospital in Tulsa with contributions from the poor and needy? Why not just heal the sick free of charge and save them a huge hospital bill? Why did these preachers always need a television camera in order to heal? Why didn't they just walk down the sidewalk healing the multitudes as Jesus did, or go room to room in a hospital? Why did the Holy Spirit always need money in order to miraculously move?

Seriously, is it really God's will for radio and television preachers to become filthy rich selling God's free grace to the sick and poor? Why do they need luxurious private jets to travel around in style telling poor people about Jesus and putting a fee on faith? Jesus walked or rode a donkey and told people about God's love for free. More and more, I saw the stark, sickening contrast between these arrogant, prideful charlatans and the humble Christ they presumably served.

It took me a while, but I finally got clear vision about these wolves dressed in their fancy, designer sheep clothing cheating poor, innocent people out of their last dime. Jesus long ago provided the answer: You can't worship God and mammon at the same time. These men who invaded our homes and lives with their polished, practiced promises of divine blessings and healing were not truly worshiping the God of glory; they were deceptively worshiping the god of greed. They are no different from the money changers at the Temple who Jesus said had changed His Father's house into a den of thieves. It was all a calculated, fraudulent deception. The prayer requests that faithful followers sent in were often thrown in the garbage while their checks were rushed to the bank.

There are some sorry, sociopathic scoundrels running loose in this world who will lie to you, cheat you, and steal your last penny without any moral compunction. I personally put these con-artists in that category. Do not be hoodwinked and victimized by them!

Eventually, a few got in trouble with the feds, such as one in the Dallas- Fort Worth area and the other whose diamond-bedecked wife had the fake, fluffy hairdo. Others are still going strong today, such as one who recently said he needed three private jets to travel the world for Jesus and was pleading for contributions.

All I can say is this: Anyone who would knowingly, willfully, and deceitfully con a trusting soul out of one penny by fraudulently promising them a blessing from God in exchange for a financial contribution is no better than Judas. May God have mercy on their soul.

Oh, before I forget, let me tell you what eventually happened with my failing vision. Around age twenty-seven, a prominent ophthalmologist in Jackson examined my blind left eye and my failing retina in my right eye and somberly told me to prepare myself for blindness. I returned to my office where I worked, closed the door, broke down crying, and cried out to God, "Lord, how am I going to live as a blind man? Please help me!" Suddenly, it was as if an angelic choir began singing to me, "Turn your eyes upon Jesus, look full in His wonderful face, and the things of earth will grow strangely dim in the light of His glory and grace." An almost surreal sense of peace flooded my anguished soul. That was nearly fifty years ago, and my vision never significantly worsened after that.

I'm still seeing today, with the aid of glasses, and I didn't have to put my hand on the radio and send Oral Roberts money to experience that amazing miracle of God's healing grace.

Getting Spanked with the Ten Commandments

Fortunately, there is no public record of my crime. I was never featured on "America's Most Wanted," but I did it. In the midst of a screaming, hair-pulling, shin-kicking twelve-year-old temper tantrum, I blurted out something to my brother that I soon regretted: I threatened to prematurely end his existence on this earth and hasten the enjoyment of his heavenly reward.

My only defense was uncontrolled impulse. You know, the kind of emotional explosion that is reserved only for the baby of the family in sibling relationships when he has been picked on and laughed at way beyond any mortal's toleration limit. It's not just a big snake that will bite you; poke at a baby snake long enough and see if he won't coil up and strike back. That describes me on the day I threatened to put an asterisk beside my brother's name on the actuarial chart of life expectancy.

Once my crime was committed, I was immediately dragged before the prosecuting attorney, judge, and jury, all of whom were combined into one little dress-wearing woman—my mother. There was no due process of law here and no presumption of innocence until proven guilty. The Constitution was about as meaningful in my situation as a tattered Sears catalog. The lady judge had heard my threat with her own ears. Why worry with more proof? I was immediately found guilty as charged.

Next came the punishment phase. There was no need to file an appeal; that would have just brought on a harsher sentence. In my frightened mind, I was already practicing running in a circle fast enough to minimize the impact of a leather belt and puckering up my little fanny cheeks. I figured the tighter I pulled the pucker string, the fewer square inches of hinny skin would be exposed to that belt.

But, to my astonishment, Judge Mama imposed a most unusual sentence: "You go get the Bible, sit down in that chair, and read the Ten Commandments out loud to me until I tell you to stop." I couldn't believe my good fortune. No blistered, red rump to worry about; just do a little Bible narration and I was free go. If this was all the punishment I was going to get, I might just threaten my brother again in the same way on another day and in another fight. I always had this feeling that I was mama's favorite child anyway, and now I knew it.

With an air of relief, I blithely fetched the old family Bible. This was no ordinary Bible. It was one of those huge old King James Bibles that contained the Old and New Testaments, a concordance, a biblical dictionary, full-page Renaissance art depictions of every event in the life of Christ, and enough family history pages to record my lineage all the way back to Adam and Eve.

So, with Genesis hanging off one side of my lap and the Revelation hanging off the other side, I began to loudly and clearly read and get my sentence out of the way. The way I saw it, this would only take a few minutes, my sin would be forgiven, I'd be redeemed, and I could go back to being angry as a wet setting-hen at my brother. But it didn't quite work out that way.

I breezed through the first reading. The second reading went a bit slower, and a few things began to pop out at me. For example, for a long time I had noticed some of the deacons would loudly shout "Amen" during the sermon, but then they would pull out a Camel, or whip out their little black packet of OCB cigarette paper, pop open a can of Prince Albert, and light up before they got to the first red oak tree in the church yard. I thought "Thou" meant them. But somewhere during the second reading, it hit me that "Thou" meant me, also. That's when it started getting personal.

During the third reading, a lump began to form in my throat, and my voice wasn't as strong and cocksure as at first. The fourth reading began the meltdown. When I read "Thou shall not kill," I fully realized that God was really unhappy with me, not to mention Judge Mama. This was some serious stuff.

Then, during about the fifth or sixth reading, the part about honoring your father and mother slapped me up beside my head. What did that actually mean? Would threatening to reduce the number of her living children by one-third constitute dishonoring my mother? And then this part really hit home: "that your days may be long on the earth." What? If this was true, it wasn't my brother that was going to vacate the premises early, it was me! This ain't right, I wanted to yell. According to these Ten Commandments, I'm on death row at twelve years of age for being angry with my brother. So, with this plaintive, quivering voice, I pleadingly asked, "Can I quit now?" Judge Mama stared at me, and firmly responded, "Keep reading!"

Then the part about remembering the Sabbath Day and keeping it holy unveiled all my Sunday crimes, like not wanting to go to church. But the worst Sunday sin was keeping some of the change mama gave me to put in the offering plate so I could buy a Slow-Poke all-day sucker from Mr. Otis and Miss Ruby Sue's grocery store.

But I had already been punished for that, or so I thought. I learned the hard way that when God is angry with you, things can quickly go wrong. After robbing God of His offering, I went to sleep during church one night on one of those old wooden pews, and I had a really bad dream that some kind of ugly, mean booger jumped off the barn roof on top of me. I started loudly moaning, kicking the back of the pew, and most of that change fell out of my pocket and hit the wooden floor in Good Hope Baptist Church. Some of the coins even rolled a few feet, like they were headed to the offering plate. When people stopped laughing, including the preacher, the stare my mama gave me made me feel like I was in the No Hope Baptist Church.

By now, I was sniffling, snorting, stuttering and could hardly pronounce the words in the Ten Commandments. I was learning stuff about myself and my sins that I never dreamed of. Did "covet" include all the good stuff my friends had that I wished I had? Did "bearing false witness against my neighbor" include the snide, unkind comments I had made about some of the other kids at school, not to mention a couple of overbearing teachers?

At this point in the penal stage, I was a crying, broken-hearted child begging for relief. This was many times worse than getting my little booty whacked with a belt. When Judge Mama realized how repentant I was, she said, "Now go hug your brother, tell him you love him, and don't ever let me hear you say that again." I was ready to do just about anything to stop reading the Ten Commandments, but hugging my brother and telling him I loved him really pushed my repentance to the limit.

Why? Because I knew when I hugged him, he would whisper in my ear, "goody, goody, that was funny," and we would start all over again. Such is the unending cycle of human anger and sin.

But I did learn one thing for sure. If reading the Ten Commandments to Judge Mama was this sobering and convicting, I sure don't want to stand before God one day and have to read them to Him. Then I realized that, because of Jesus' death on the cross and my faith in Him as Lord and Savior, I won't have to. Jesus taught me that the Ten Commandments are not just principles of religious law chiseled in stone, they are spiritual instructions on how to truly love God and love my neighbor as myself. Jesus turned the Ten Commandments from a cause of punishment into a reason for praise!

I just wish Judge Mama had seen them that way, too.

I Don't Speak Algebra

Two significant forces shaped my decision-making process when I graduated from Purvis High School in 1966. The first was my passionate dislike for dairy farming and my consuming determination never again to handle those four, fleshy milk faucets hanging under a Holstein cow. I had to get away from the farm, and whatever college I attended had to be far enough away that I couldn't commute.

The second controlling force was my total inability to understand math above a basic level. I have great respect for mathematicians, but I just don't speak algebra. I know that's a play on words, but it accurately conveys my dysfunctional math ability. How I passed Algebra I in high school, while setting still-unbroken absentee records, is attributable to God's grace and the generous, compassionate grading of my math teacher, and not to my ability and understanding.

So, when I looked at basic degree requirements in every college and junior college, I ran smack into that dreaded monster that threatened to deny me a college education and possibly send me back to the dairy farm—college algebra. "Oh, cursed thing, why tormentest thou me?" If Shakespeare didn't have a line like that, he should have.

But the vision of again fondling those four, fleshy faucets kept me doggedly searching for an alternative. Finally, I looked at a liberal arts program at Ole Miss that allowed a student to take two additional science courses, such as botany, in lieu of college algebra, and there was my answer. So, off to Ole Miss I went, and I kissed the memory of four, fleshy milk faucets and that demon algebra goodbye.

In my seventy-five years, I have attained some limited success in life, all without knowing if A plus B really does equal C. Throughout twenty years as a pastor, I never found a biblical account where Moses said, "If I only could figure out why X plus Y equals Z, then I could get the Israelites across the deep Red Sea!"

Missing two or three days of school a week obviously didn't help any, as I have previously described to you, but I was as lost in Algebra I as a blind goose in an Artic blizzard, and it had no meaningful application to my life back then. Never once did I squat under a big Holstein cow and stare at those four black and white milk spickets and ponder if a polynomial would make milk come out easier.

But, here's what the Lord did with my inability to understand math. He opened a door for me to attend Ole Miss, since that was my only option. There, I not only earned a B.A. degree and a law degree, but I also met people whom God later used to open even more doors of opportunity for me. This may sound a bit strange, but in truth much of my academic and professional attainment stems from the fact that I don't speak algebra and how God used that to shape and channel my life.

He can do the same for you. God can take your greatest weakness and your worst fear and slowly but surely use it in a way that will amaze you and bring glory to Him. Even if you don't speak algebra like me, or you're not as gifted as others, you are not a failure! Stop looking at how many times you've failed, and instead triumphantly run the race that is before you. You may just discover that X plus Y equals V...ictory!

The Fear of a Quitter

This is not a self-indulgent pity party, nor am I seeking sympathy. Rather, I'm unlocking some emotions securely sealed away for over fifty-five years in hopes it might encourage others. I want to tell you what it feels like to be a quitter and to give up on life at fifteen years of age.

I honestly don't know what I was thinking back then. In reality, I wasn't thinking. Instead, I gave in to the deepest fears a child can have. When I was nine, my parents divorced, resulting in deep family bitterness. I was caught in the middle of a heated family war, and I was no longer able to see people I loved, which I didn't understand. I never saw my Grandmother Voss again.

Our small, struggling dairy farm became the responsibility of my two older brothers and me, ages 17, 13, and 9, along with my mother. By the time I was 15, one brother had entered the military, and the farm operation was just my oldest brother and me.

Quite frankly, it was a hellish, nightmare experience. I was always working, seven days a week and usually until 9:00 or 10:00 at night, whether in blistering heat, freezing cold, or pouring rain and never receiving any reward, compensation, or even a thank you. No one ever asked whether I was happy, which I wasn't. Basically, I saw myself as little more than a child slave.

As a result, I missed a tremendous amount of school working on the farm. I always felt behind, and I seldom had homework done on time. What child wants to do homework late at night when they're hungry, dirty, and too tired to even hold their head up?

I dreaded going to school. I was terrified of being called on in class, because I was seldom prepared. I began to feel greatly inferior to others, even though I faked being friendly. I became afraid of close relationships out of fear of being hurt and rejected. I felt different, poor, and alone, with no close bond with anyone.

I retreated into a fantasy world. I read every horse book in the Purvis library that mama would check out, and I pretended to be one of those book characters. I wanted to be anyone other than me, and to live anywhere but on that farm.

In the ninth grade, I just gave up. I didn't care anymore, and I quit school. I hated going anywhere, especially school, and being seen. Overcome with crushing insecurity and inferiority feelings, I was screaming for help inside, and no one heard me.

But, quitting only made matters worse because I realized I would never be anything but a failure, and I would never experience the life others would. I knew I would always be poor and uneducated. Increasingly, I shied away from human contact. I would hide each day when the school bus came by so they would not see me out working, and I would even hide from relatives who came to visit. My life consisted of milking cows and working in the mud, and I truly felt hopeless.

One morning, as if he were an angel sent from God, one of my teachers, Mack Avery, called and talked encouragingly to me. Begging me to return to school, he assured me I could do it. I was terrified to go back, but after thinking about it a couple of days, I returned to Purvis High School after being out for about six weeks.

I wish I could say that my attendance record became perfect, but work on the dairy farm only got more demanding. During my sophomore year, I missed sixty-eight days of school, but at least I was enrolled. There were multiple weeks in which I attended school only one or two days. My junior and senior years were a little better, but not by much. I've jokingly said I had all A's in high school—for being absent. There was no compulsory attendance law back in those days, in case you're wondering. Finally, in the Spring of 1966, I graduated. Needless to say, I was not the valedictorian. Some people graduate Cum Laude or Magna Cum Laude because of their superior grades. I've said I graduated Oh My Laude—I actually made it!

Here's my point and purpose in sharing these memories: We have no idea what forces are working in someone else's mind...their fears, their failures, or their struggles with physical and emotional pressures that dominate them. It deeply troubles me to hear someone judge another person and criticize or condemn them, especially a young person. It is sheer arrogance and cruelty in my opinion.

Instead, why can't we strive to be a source of encouragement to others? Why can't we build others up with the same zeal we employ in tearing them down? If we are Christians, why can't we bear one another's burdens, as we are taught to do, rather than driving someone deeper into the despair of failure? Of all the people in my life when I became a high school dropout, only one truly encouraged me to crawl out of the hole of hopelessness and achieve greater things in life.

If you could see a picture of me then, you would see only a shy, dirty, young boy wearing ragged clothes with tractor grease and cow waste all over me. But would you also see someone who would go from being a ninth-grade grade dropout to eventually earning a B.A. degree and a Juris Doctor degree from Ole Miss and a Master of Divinity degree from New Orleans Baptist Theological Seminary because one person stepped into his despair and encouraged him to believe he could succeed?

Looking at my picture, you would see failure and fear. But would you also see the self-confidence that this dirty kid would one day have to be Vice President and General Counsel of Mississippi Baptist Health Systems, one of the largest hospital systems in Mississippi?

The picture would show you a young boy who would run and hide in fear and shame even from relatives. But would you also see a preacher of the gospel who could fearlessly and passionately preach to hundreds of people?

Would your eyes rest on the image of a failing ninth grader or a published author?

The answer is none of you would see that, because one's ultimate potential is never clearly seen. Admittedly, there may be evidence of it, but not its full magnitude.

And therein is the joyous challenge of the ministry of encouragement. When you compassionately reach out to a hurting individual, you have no idea what you're ultimately dealing with, and it may be years, or even decades, before you see results, but you will have planted the seed of hope and started its growth. You just have to believe that there's something in every person that's better, higher, and holier than what's present before you, and you patiently strive to bring that out in them.

I don't know what Mack Avery saw in me, but it was something greater than being a quitter and a failure, and I am eternally grateful. Being a devoted and caring teacher, as he was with me, is one of the highest callings a person can have.

Let me encourage you to become a comparable source of encouragement in someone's life today. Let them know they might not climb to the top rung on the ladder of their dreams, but encourage them to climb to the top rung on the ladder of their abilities. You have no idea what change you may help bring about in their life.

For some personal and private reason, you may have become a quitter yourself. I don't have to tell you the feelings you are experiencing, for you know them all too well. Let me encourage you to keep trying. Renew your goals, strengthen your resolve, and dig deeper for greater determination. You can do this. There are more people than you realize who believe in you. God never designed you nor designated you to be a quitter and a failure. And, more than anything, realize that Jesus, your Friend and Encourager, always has your back.

The Beatitudes[1]

Introduction

The Sermon on the Mount begins with eight statements by Jesus, known as the Beatitudes, which are cherished by Christians and viewed as principles by which a believer experiences the blessedness of the Christian life. Even though "beatitude" does not appear in the Bible, the term is derived from the Latin word *beatitudo*, which describes an experience of blessedness. In general literary terms, beatitudes are statements that begin with "blessed" or "happy" and then describe the human trait or emotion that merits the status of blessedness. As a general form of expression, beatitude type statements may be found throughout the Bible (Ps.1:1; 119:1-2; Rev. 22:14).

Jesus said to His disciples, "These things I have spoken to you, that My joy my remain in you, and that your joy may be full" (John 15:11). The joy that Jesus described results from the fulfillment of something that brings great delight to an individual, especially of a spiritual nature. It is not the same as physical happiness, but rather the attainment of a goal, a purpose, or the meaning of a relationship. Jesus could not have always been physically happy, given all that He experienced, but He always experienced great delight and joy in His unbroken relationship with God. It was this joy and blessedness that He wanted His disciples to experience. The Beatitudes, therefore, describe the necessary steps of repentant faith that each Christian must take in order to enter into His joy.

The Beatitudes are unparalleled in biblical literature for their meaning and importance in transforming joyless, obligatory religious ritual into true happiness about one's relationship with God. The Beatitudes must be examined not only in their relationship to Jesus' demand for repentance, but also in terms of how Jesus instructed His disciples about the inner spiritual transformation of repentance that brings about such blessedness. As a master teacher, Jesus not only told His disciples about the absolute necessity of repentance, but He also explained to them the spiritual mechanics of the transformation process, and then promised a resulting joyous spiritual experience never before known to them.

---

[1] The study of the Beatitudes was first published in *A Sermon on a Mountainside*. They were later modified slightly and shared in a Facebook devotional series reproduced for this book.

Jesus was supremely blessed by God, experienced a consummate peace with God, and knew a sense of joy that He invited His disciples to share. Yet the gospels do not record that Jesus ever laughed, shouted for joy, sang or expressed His joy in any physical manner. His joy was not based on and expressed through physical happiness or emotional exuberance. That does not mean that He was a dour and sullen man, but rather one who realized an inner happiness and joy of such magnitude that it radiated from Him and required no other physical expression. Jesus did not pursue happiness in the way that His disciples, both then and now, traditionally view happiness, yet He is the single source of spiritual blessedness, happiness, and joy that many spend their life searching for.

It is important to realize that blessedness described by Jesus in the Beatitudes is not a defined status that one earns, but rather is a spiritual state that one receives through repentance, faith, and grace that progressively grows, just as Jesus described in the parable of the mustard seed (Matt. 13:31). It is a spiritual reality in which all the ancient covenant promises of God to His people are fulfilled and given life in the believer through faith in Jesus. It is the very joy experienced by Jesus himself in His relationship with God that can neither be earned by human effort nor diminished by worldly circumstances.

The transcendent joy of the kingdom of heaven is therefore experienced inwardly and is created by divine grace through the presence of the Holy Spirit in the believer's life. Consequently, Jesus proclaimed a new relationship with God, higher and holier than any prior experience that man had known, in which a believer experiences an ever-increasing peace with God, a profound sense of spiritual comfort, and fulfillment of one's deepest hunger for the righteousness of God. Jesus described that overall experience as "blessed."

Blessedness should never be considered solely as an experience of physical joy, for such happiness is dependent on positive circumstances. Rather, it is an inner fulfillment and wholeness neither gained from, nor diminished by, physical events and circumstances surrounding the believer. By covenant faith in Jesus, it is the life of God implanted in the believer and nurtured by the Holy Spirit that is so spiritually complete and fulfilling in Jesus that it is impossible to fathom any other thing that would enhance the experience, and thus it brings total delight to the believer. This is the nature of life that Jesus desires to give to every Christian and to the covenant church as a whole.

The Beatitudes are the fundamental concepts of how one experiences a transformed spiritual attitude toward God and others that enables him to fully inherit the kingdom of heaven and to experience the joyous "blessedness" of Jesus. Collectively, they are the key to the happiness of Christian living.

The Beatitudes

Blessed are the poor in spirit, for theirs is the kingdom of heaven (Matt. 5:3).

Jesus began the Sermon on the Mount with a statement so implausible to his Jewish listeners that it would have been laughable—had it not been true. All who listened to Jesus' sermon were amazed at His wisdom, but surely they were startled by His opening statement because it would have been considered impossible.

Since the beginning of Jewish history, heaven had been viewed as the exclusive domain of God. Among the many Old Testament references to heaven, the following statements validate the universal belief in Israel that heaven was the distinct domain of God:

- Heaven was God's creation (Gen. 2:4).
- God was the "Possessor" of heaven (Gen. 14: 19).
- God spoke to His people from heaven (Exod. 20:22).
- Heaven was God's dwelling place (I Kings 8:30).
- God heard the penitent prayers of His people from heaven (II Chron. 7:14).
- He is the God of heaven (Neh. 2:4).
- God's throne is in heaven (Psalm 11:4).
- God looks down on His creation from heaven (Psalm 33:13).
- God opens the windows of heaven and pours out blessings on His people (Mal. 3:10).

In Jewish thought, the heavenly habitation of God was so beyond human understanding that attempts to describe its nature and location were ambiguous at best. Visualized and understood only through physical observation of the heavenly heights, God resided higher than the visible clouds and the domain of soaring birds. Likewise, God was greater, higher, and holier than the realm of the sun, moon, and stars. As a result, belief in a "third heaven" developed which was inhabited by God and was beyond all known creation. Jesus referred to it as "My Father's house" (John 14:2).

Consequently, since heaven belonged exclusively to God, an individual had little expectation of experiencing the full nature of God's heavenly realm. Therefore, many who heard Jesus say that the kingdom of heaven could be theirs would have considered the statement preposterous. But it was a divine promise of inheritance and entitlement made not to a nation, but to every individual who possessed the spiritual characteristics described by Jesus.

Not only was the idea of having a personal vested right in God's heavenly domain incomprehensible, but the manner in which it would be obtained was equally shocking. The heritage of Israel was based on the presumption that righteousness was gained through obedience to the religious law and its rules and ritual. It had been that way for hundreds of years, and no prophet had ever stated otherwise.

Therefore, Jesus faced the great challenge of convincing His disciples that the kingdom of heaven could not be earned by personal merit but only received as a gift of divine grace. Consequently, Jesus voiced one of the most fundamental concepts of repentance in one simple expression, "Blessed are the poor in spirit, for theirs is the kingdom of heaven."

The Greek concept of poverty was most often expressed through two words, *penes* and *ptochos*. Penes described a poor man who had very little and subsisted on meager essentials for life. *Ptochos*, on the other hand, described one who literally had nothing, and the distinction is crucial in understanding Jesus' statement. The poor man who had little (*penes*) still looked unto himself to earn his meager livelihood, while the poor man who had nothing (*ptochos*) had no possessions whatsoever and neither had the means of obtaining anything—and the reality of nothing cannot be overly emphasized in this concept.

Whereas the poor man with a little still relied on himself in some way, the poor man with nothing did not. He had lost all thought of self-reliance and therefore cast all his hope and expectation on the mercy, compassion, and generosity of another to help him. He was a beggar in the truest sense of the word, for his capacity to live came from another and not from himself.

So it is with a sinner who turns to Jesus in faith. Through this beatitude, Jesus proclaimed the radical new concept that entrance into heaven has nothing to do with one's own worth, self-righteous efforts of goodness, and compliance with religious law and ritual, but rather is entirely dependent on the mercy, grace, and compassion of God.

In order to better grasp the magnitude of Jesus' statement, one should contrast it with the arrogance, pride, and presumed self-worth that characterized the religious leadership of Israel. Based on Jesus' descriptions of them, they gloated over their positions and cherished their public status, "…for they loved the praise of men more than the praise of God" (John 12:43). Many were obsessed with the attainment of personal riches as physical proof of their righteous status with God and how blessed they were, causing them to become "lovers of money" (Luke 16:14).

Religious worship was a public performance with the required daily prayers being said on street corners in open view and charitable deeds being done "in order to be seen by men" (Matt. 6:1). Jesus viewed all of these self- glorifying acts as pure hypocrisy.

Jesus faced the extremely difficult challenge of changing the historic mind-set of Israel that the kingdom of heaven is not earned based on one's self-worth or religious works. It is a gift from God, and the less on sees his own entitlement to the heavenly kingdom as a reward for religious work and sees it more as a gift of grace from God, the greater will be his understanding of the blessedness of his heavenly inheritance.

Thus, true repentance must begin with one's own sense of worthiness to be in the presence of God. Since the beginning of God's covenant with Abraham, God has "reckoned" a person to be righteous on the basis of faith alone (Gen. 15:6). Repentance, therefore, forces one to inventory all of his personal works that presumably obligate God to consider him righteous and accept that the balance is zero. It is the process by which one totally removes himself from the process and allows God alone to allocate righteousness, rather than considering its attainment to be a joint venture between God and himself.

When one finally understands that the kingdom of heaven is a divine, spiritual gift from God and not a religious commodity to be bought, and accepts their complete spiritual poverty before God, then—and only then—can they finally abandon self-righteous law and understand grace. Repentance enables one to humbly stand in the presence of God with nothing and receive unlimited eternal blessings, rather than proudly standing in His presence with presumed self-made riches, and boasting of self-righteous works, and discovering their value merits nothing.

The fundamental tenant of Christianity is salvation by grace through faith (Eph. 2:8), and it is no different with inheritance of the kingdom of heaven. Not one square inch of God's heavenly domain can be purchased by earthly human works. Its entirety will be given by God to those who understand their own unworthiness to receive citizenship within the kingdom, to those who faithfully believe that Jesus alone makes them an heir to the kingdom, and to those who give God total credit for granting this immeasurable gift of heavenly citizenship to them.

It is one of the great paradoxes of the age-old human quest to attain immortality and understanding of God: Those who proudly anticipate their reward for works of religious superiority receive nothing; whereas those who give up all hope of gaining the kingdom of heaven through prideful self-righteous effort and who cast all their hope and expectation upon God through faith in Jesus receive it all. Oh, the indescribable blessedness and joy of poor spiritual beggars who look only unto Jesus and not unto themselves, for the kingdom of heaven belongs only to them!

Thoughts to ponder:

1. Describe your sense of spiritual poverty.

2. Do you focus more on the values of your Christian character or your spiritual poverty?

3. Does your sense of spiritual poverty make you feel depressed or fill you with the experience of joy and blessedness?

Blessed are those who mourn, for they shall be comforted (Matt. 5:4).

To what degree does sincere sorrow and contrition for personal sin reflect true repentance? The answer reveals the meaning of this beatitude. Repentance from sin is turning away from one's past and present sinful action and turning toward a life that glorifies God. It is the transition from the sorrow of evil to the joy of divine goodness. Repentance and contrition must be motivated by a sincere conviction that one's actions are an affront to God's holiness, resulting in true personal sorrow and remorse. As a result, one humbles himself before God in confession of his sins, experiences a deep heart-felt desire to turn from them, and expresses a sincere plea to God for forgiveness. True spiritual sorrow—and not feigned emotionalism—is a basic barometer of the sincerity of one's repentance.

But what if a sinner is not truly sorry for his sins? Can one repent from something for which he has no regret? As long as he is blameless in his own eyes, inner attitudes of pride, boastfulness, anger, hatred, and prejudice do not matter, and thus he may feel blameless and have no sorrow for a cold heart and mean spirit. How can a person repent from such ungodly feelings if he sees nothing wrong with them, since they are a basic part of his life?

Jesus frequently confronted people, particularly the scribes and Pharisees, who viewed themselves as righteous because they fanatically kept the religious rules and ritual, but were spiritually corrupt. The gospel accounts provide little indication, however, that any of them manifested any deep, sincere sorrow and contrition for their guilt of personal sin.

The Pharisees and scribes in particular, and the Sadducees to a lesser extent, were very emotional about their religious beliefs, even theatrical at times. Throughout the gospels, one finds them manifesting a wide range of emotions and gestures to dramatize their fervor in defending the law. For example, the Pharisees and scribes expressed great indignation that Jesus would heal on the Sabbath (Mark 3:1-6, Matt. 12:14), pluck grains of wheat on the Sabbath (Matt. 12:2), or befriend sinners and tax collectors by dining with them (Luke 15:12, Matt. 9:11). Likewise, the High Priest appeared distraught and tore his garments at Jesus' statement that He was the Son of God (Mark 14:63).

However, there is no indication that any of them felt remorse for their sins against God, or for their cold, indifferent attitudes toward others. Also, there isn't an instance where a Pharisee or scribe asked God to forgive his sins, yet they were the ones who publicly held themselves up as role models of righteousness.

Thus, Jesus transitioned religion from an impersonal obedience of law, rules, and regulations that glorified man to a personal covenant of love in one's life that glorified God. Through Jesus, religion became a one-on-one relationship with God as one's heavenly Father (Matt. 6:9), and it was no longer defined by law but rather by love for God and others.

Sin also took on a new meaning, for it now encompassed far more than what one merely did physically in disobedience to the law and instead included what one felt and thought in his heart, mind, and soul, and it redefined the spiritual consequences of disobedience.

Adultery, for example, was no longer just a technical definition under the law, but rather what a man felt when he looked at a woman with such desire that, in his head and in his heart, he had already committed himself to the act of adultery and now sought only the opportunity (Matt. 5:27-28). In like manner, Jesus defined murder as primarily involving attitudes of the heart, not just actions of the hand (Matt. 5:21-22).

Consequently, Jesus ushered in the realization that sin is a personal act that offends God and deeply grieves the Holy Spirit. Sin was no longer just the transgression of a religious rule, but rather the transgression of the righteousness of God, and as a consequence, one ought to feel a deep personal sense of grief and remorse over intentional acts and attitudes that literally grieve the Spirit of God. Jesus described it as an intense mourning (*pentheo*), such as when a close friend or family member dies.

However, those who do mourn will be comforted, for in their grief they will not only turn away in repentance from the sin that so grieves God and themselves, but they will also find the blessedness of relief and forgiveness from the heart of merciful God. This beatitude promise of divine comfort is one of the most succinct summations of Christian theology in the New Testament, for it introduces the ultimate atoning work of Jesus and the work of the Holy Spirit in the believer's life that produces true spiritual comfort, hence the name "Comforter" or "Helper" (John 14:16).

The Comforter is sent by Jesus to seal one's salvation and to sanctify and equip the believer with spiritual gifts and abilities that glorify God. Through implanting the life of Jesus in the believer, the Comforter becomes the guarantor of the truth of God through Jesus for each believer and thus assures the forgiveness of sin, the promise of eternal life, and citizenship within the kingdom of heaven. As a result, every true Christian enters into God's eternal rest and divine comfort (Heb. 4:1).

Comfort is what God does for believers through mercy and grace, not what one creates for himself. Historically, repentance and comfort are joint concepts in Old Testament theology, for they are derived from the same word and are inseparable. Comfort is the central theme of Isaiah 40 and Isaiah 51 and was the blessing granted to Israel when she repented and returned to God. It is through repentance that one is enabled to totally receive the love, mercy, and grace of God through Jesus as Lord and Savior, and experience the indwelling of the Holy Spirit who grants to us the very comfort of God, for it is God who said, "I, even I, am He who comforts you" (Isa. 51:12).

Through faith in Jesus, and the presence of the Comforter in one's life, every Christian is assured of the forgiveness of sin and guaranteed everlasting life. His once sinful life is redeemed back to God and given the righteousness of God by grace through faith; he is adopted as a child of God and made a joint heir with Jesus in the fullness of every heavenly blessing; sanctified and set apart through the power of the Holy Spirit in the holiness of God; given direct access to God through the priesthood of Jesus; given the assurance that nothing will separate the believer from the love of God; given a peace that passes all understanding; and experiences an everlasting life filled with continuous praise and thanksgiving to God for His mercy, love, and grace revealed through Jesus. The work of the Comforter is to bring the mournful believer into the fullness of this divine spiritual comfort. It is the blessed life of those who inherit the kingdom of heaven, and it begins the moment one repents and prepares for the way of the Lord in his life. The nature of this life is "comfort."

Oh, the blessedness of those whose heart is mournfully broken in sorrow and contrition over their sin against God, for, through their faith in Jesus, they shall joyfully enter into the eternal comfort of God.

Thoughts to ponder:

1. Have you ever been burdened over your sins against God to the point that you grieved over them as you would grieve over the loss of a friend or loved one?

2. Do you find yourself asking God to "forgive my sins" without ever really considering what they are and how they grieve the Holy Spirit?

3. Are you burdened by your unholy attitudes toward others that may be hidden in the confines of your heart and known only to you, or do you simply view them as a part of your life and you are not bothered by them?

4. Are you willing to give up every action and attitude you can think of that grieves the Holy Spirit and never allow those to define your Christian life again, and are you willing to make that one of your highest prayer priorities?

5. Can you describe an instance in your life where you experienced the Holy Spirit's presence providing you with spiritual help, comfort, and peace?

Blessed are the meek, for they shall inherit the earth (Matt. 5:5).

When Jesus began proclaiming the need for repentance, He encountered a religious culture that resisted change and tenaciously clung to established worship ritual. The "tradition of the elders" (Matt. 15:2-3) was of greater importance than any prophetic plea for reform. The most noticeable trait of Israel's religious culture was an intractable refusal by its religious leaders to even hear and consider any new revelation of truth about God. Even though He amazed them with the nature of His wisdom, nevertheless, Jesus was often ridiculed and reviled for His teaching.

At the heart of Israel's sin, as it is with all mankind, was a prideful, insatiable desire to seek greater gratification for one's physical desires than for one's spiritual nature. It is far easier to climb down the spiritual ladder toward temptation than to climb up the ladder toward consecration to God. But, the heart of God's love and grace always beckons one up to a higher spiritual plane where one's desire for God is greater than his physical desire for himself.

Consequently, Jesus insisted that every believer totally submit his own personal will to the control, domination, and sovereignty of God, and He personally demonstrated the vital relationship between the will of God and the work of God through His life and ministry. In doing so, a Christian does not lose the power of his personality; rather, he channels the power of his personhood into a fundamentally different direction as determined by the divine will and purpose of God. He moves from the shifting sand of human emotions to the rock-hard stability of divine direction in his life.

Jesus sought a way to free Christians from themselves and eternally link them to the divine will of His heavenly Father and the guidance and power of the Holy Spirit. That would require a radical new way of thinking about themselves and a dynamic new way of envisioning their relationship with God. In order to accomplish this, Jesus chose to describe to them the blessedness of those who are "meek."

Jesus masterfully used everyday circumstances as powerful teaching tools, and the concept of meekness is one of those. *Praus* (meek, gentle, mild) was a term often used to describe an animal that had been "broken" for domestic use, particularly a horse or donkey. It did not mean that the horse's spirit was broken and he was rendered lifeless and lazy. Conversely, the once wild and uncontrollable animal, although still possessing all his drive and power, had been "gentled."

There is a vast difference between being broken and being gentled. If the spirit of a horse is truly broken, then he has no desire to do anything and responds only when forced to act. He may be prodded into action, but he has no heart for it. However, when the spirit of that animal is gentled or "meeked" by a caring, patient master through the process of training and preparation, the wild, uncontrolled actions are indeed curtailed, but all the drive, power and stamina of that animal are preserved and yielded over to the controlling hands of his master through faith and trust. All of the fighting, kicking, biting, and bucking are gone, and the animal experiences an inner peace, or gentleness, based on total submission to his master, without giving up one ounce of power and potential. It is then that the horse is "meeked," and it is only through this meekness that his true potential is achieved. His wild past is gone, but his future will now be greater than anything he ever knew before, for he is now controlled by a person, power, and purpose infinitely greater and wiser than himself. He will never again be the same.

Surely Jesus saw a wild horse or donkey gentled in this manner, and He saw meekness not as a personality trait defined by a mild mannered, unassertive personality, but rather as the character and personality of one who has yielded all of his desire and motivation to God. His spirit is not broken; rather, it has been "gentled" by the loving power of the Holy Spirit, and all of his personal ability is now channeled away from himself and directed toward God and others, as guided by the Spirit of God.

Jesus was the meekest man who ever lived, but He was also the most powerful, resolute, focused and determined man who ever lived. His life was totally yielded in trust and faith to the will of God, and it produced power and purpose, as well as an inner peace and gentleness, which transcended the turmoil of life around him. That is the life He desires each of His followers to experience.

Jesus promised that the meek "shall inherit the earth." He did not mean the physical planet, but rather a broader and deeper inheritance with a rich spiritual meaning. There are numerous Old Testament promises that God's covenant people would "inherit the land." Rooted in the divine promise of the Promised Land, inheritance of the land signified the blessings of the righteous within a divine realm prepared for them. The poetic promises of Psalm 37 are good examples:

- Those who wait on the Lord shall inherit the earth (v. 9).
- The meek shall inherit the earth (v. 11).
- Those blessed by God shall inherit the earth (v. 22).
- The righteous shall inherit the land (v. 29).

It is interesting how Jesus drew directly from the promises of this Psalm for this beatitude. The spiritual concept of the inheritance of the kingdom of heaven and the inheritance of the earth are synonymous. The fullness of the kingdom will be inherited by those who fully surrender their life to the controlling authority of God through active and faithful obedience to Jesus and who follow Him under the guidance of the Holy Spirit. God's will becomes their work and is accomplished through the dynamic power of meekness. As a result, they inherit life within the kingdom of the redeemed—the eternal spiritual land wherein all the promises of God are fulfilled.

Thoughts to ponder:

1. Apart from your profession of faith in Jesus and your baptism, has there ever been a moment in your life when you totally surrendered your personal will and desire for life to God's will and purpose for you?

2. Are you willing to go anywhere, do anything, surrender any personal treasure, or bear any hardship in submission to His purpose in your life?

3. Could you write a description of how meekness, as discussed in this study, characterizes your Christian life?

Blessed are those who hunger and thirst for righteousness, for they shall be filled (Matt.5:6)

Righteousness is the characteristic of God graciously given to man which enables him to experience God on a personal level and to have fellowship with Him. Righteousness describes the inherent nature and character of God, and since God is eternally perfect, pure, and sinless, He is also eternally "right" in all His ways. The righteousness of God is the cornerstone of faith, the basis of eternal divine truth, the ultimate standard for all human conduct and social order, the fundamental character of a godly man and a godly nation, and the basis on which the final redemption and judgment of mankind will be premised.

Sin is unrighteousness, and we are all sinners. Thus, in our carnal state, we are all unrighteous and separated from God. Only through the righteousness of God given to us as an act of God's grace, based on our faith in Jesus, can we stand in God's presence free and forgiven of sin. But it is Jesus' righteousness and not our own that matters. So, we are all on equal footing as sinners, and none of us have bragging rights about our own self-righteous worth, for our own efforts are of no value. Therefore, the question facing every believer is how much of God's righteous life do we really want? Tragically, history reflects that many do not want all of it. Israel wanted to be blessed by God, but showed little interest in being a blessing to other nations. Every Christian desires to be saved; but not every Christian desires to serve.

Jesus taught His disciples that repentance required a renewed desire for the fullness of God's righteousness, not just the portions that met their preconceived spiritual mindset. By describing the intensity of this spiritual desire in terms of a physical hunger for food and water, Jesus drew upon an ancient scriptural example describing the intensity with which one should desire the righteousness of God. In an arid land, one would experience extreme thirst occasionally, and David had centuries earlier poetically compared his desire for God to that of a thirsty animal craving life sustaining water:

> "As the deer pants for the water
> brooks, So pants my soul for
> You, O God.
> My soul thirsts for God,
> for the living God…" (Psalm 42:1-2).

If there is a thirst for righteousness, then likewise there is a spiritual hunger for God. It is Jesus' promise that whoever hungers and thirsts for God's righteousness will find total fulfillment in Him. However, when Jesus looked at Israel's history and the lack of commitment to the righteous nature of God's redeeming love, He realized that a higher level of commitment from Christian disciples would be needed in order to manifest the true nature of God's redeeming love to all people of the world. Therefore, in teaching about repentance and preparing for the way of the Lord in one's life, He demanded a spiritual hunger for the righteousness of God that transcended all other desires in life.

The word for hunger in this beatitude (*peinao*) is related to the word for "poor" (*penes*), and it is not the hunger of one who can readily satisfy his craving through his own resources. Rather, it is the hunger of a starving, impoverished man who is virtually unrestrained in his desire for food. He can never satisfy his hunger by his own efforts because of his poverty, and when graciously given food, he wants all he can get. He does not want just a portion; he wants all of it! It does not mean that he is greedy or gluttonous, but rather that he sees the food not only as a chance to sustain his life, but also as an opportunity to transform his life from impending death to abundant sustenance, and it is the magnitude of that opportunity that he wants to seize to the maximum extent.

It is not just the taste of the food, but the transformation of his life that the food will produce that he hungers for. Applied to the righteousness of God, it is the image of one who knows his inability to attain God's righteousness through his own self-righteous effort, and when freely offered the righteousness of God through grace by faith, he hungers and thirsts for all he can get.

It was this constant hunger and thirst to do the righteous will of His father that sustained Jesus. In response to His disciples urging Him to eat, Jesus once said, "I have food to eat of which you do not know" (John 4:32). Surprised, they asked if anyone had brought Him food, and Jesus responded, "My food is to do the will of Him who sent Me, and to finish His work" (John 4:34). He hungered for the full righteousness of His Father in His earthly life, and the knowledge that He had finished God's redeeming work.

In order for repentance to be real, one's hunger for God's righteousness and redeeming love must be as intense as that of a starving man who sees the opportunity to be so abundantly fed that his hunger and thirst are totally satisfied forever and his life thereby eternally transformed. Given that opportunity, he wants all that he can get. When one hungers and thirsts for God's righteousness with that same intensity through covenant faith in Jesus, he "shall be filled."

That short phrase marvelously describes the abundant grace of God, for it means "to feed or fatten" and is derived from the description of a feeding place overflowing with abundance. It is the imagery of fattened cattle grazing in a pasture of lush, green grass that never withers, and thus they are completely and continuously filled and never hunger again. Whoever hungers and thirsts for the fullness of God's righteousness through faith in Jesus will be totally filled spiritually in the same way.

Thoughts to ponder:

1. There is a powerful hymnal stanza which states, "When He shall come with trumpet sound, oh, may I then in Him be found; dressed in His righteousness alone, faultless to stand before the throne." Could you describe how this verse summarizes your Christian faith?

2. At some time, you have probably been very hungry and very thirsty. You may have even experienced physical weakness from lack of food or

dehydration. In that moment, you were consumed by your desire for food or water. Have you ever desired God's righteousness to that same degree so that you could be filled with His righteous nature more fully, in order to do His righteous work more completely, and reveal His redeeming love to others more sincerely?

3. Slowly repeat these words: "Fill my cup, Lord; I lift it up Lord; come and quench this thirsting of my soul. Bread of Heaven, feed me till I want no more. Fill my cup, fill it up and make me whole." These words from the great old hymn "Fill My Cup, Lord" capture the essence of this beatitude. Do they describe your desire for the righteousness of God?

Blessed are the merciful, for they shall obtain mercy (Matt. 5:7).

The Bible reveals at least three great concepts about God's eternal nature: love, mercy, and grace. Each is crucial in understanding God's redemptive power in the world, and He generously reveals the magnitude of each one in a variety of ways. One may think of the three in this way: Love is who God is, mercy is what God feels, and grace is what God does.

Divine mercy involves far more than just withholding punishment. Mercy, as described in both the Old and New Testaments, is different from the word's contemporary concept, for God's mercy is not just sympathy for sinners, but rather a deep and intensely personal brooding that compels God to act in order to save. That concept is critically important in understanding God's merciful efforts to redeem sinners and in understanding the nature of repentance taught by Jesus. God's empathy for man and His willingness to save and redeem are limitless, as revealed by Jesus' death on the cross.

The Hebrew word *chesed* is used in the Old Testament to describe mercy, but it is difficult to define and understand. Whether one defines *chesed* as mercy, compassion, pity, unfailing love, or lovingkindness, it still only partially captures the magnitude of God's mercy. But perhaps an imprecise definition is actually a good starting point, for if one begins the study of God's mercy by realizing that it is beyond human comprehension and then follows the progression of mercy to the unfathomable sacrifice of Jesus on the cross, one can better understand Jesus' demand that the mercy shown by His followers be a reflection of the indefinable mercy of God toward man. In the final analysis, God's mercy cannot be defined; it can only be experienced and shared, and that alone provides the greatest comprehension of its nature and magnitude.

The New Testament concept of mercy (*eleos*) is similar to the Hebrew idea. It is not just an unattached feeling of sympathy, but rather an active involvement in alleviating or eliminating suffering and misery caused by harmful circumstances, as manifested by a personal willingness to identify with the plight of those in need and take their suffering upon one's self. It is compassion and pity of such intensity that one is irresistibly compelled to act in order to bring healing and relief to the weary and hurting. God's mercy is a deep, compassionate brooding over the sinful circumstances of man of such intensity that it compels God to personally identify with man and take upon Himself the suffering caused by sin.

It is revealing to study the various pleas for help that people in diverse circumstances cried out to Jesus as He journeyed through Israel. Consider the following examples:

1. The plea of two blind men, "Son of David, have mercy on us!" (Matt. 9:27).

2. The cry of a mother with a demon possessed daughter, "Have mercy on me, O Lord, Son of David..." (Matt. 15:22).

3. The request of a father with an epileptic son, "Lord, have mercy on my son..." (Matt. 17:15).

4. The ten lepers, standing afar off, who pleaded, "Jesus, Master, have mercy on us!" (Luke 17:13).

5. The blind man near Jericho crying out, "Jesus, Son of David, have mercy on me!" (Luke 18:38).

It is obvious from these pleas —and there were many others—that a pervasive sense of desperation existed among the people, for the needy in Israel suffered greatly. Jesus encountered multitudes of people begging for help, and what He saw and heard moved Him deeply.

The language of the New Testament often affords meaningfully clear insight into the underlying human emotions in a situation. The gospels state that Jesus was frequently "moved with compassion" as He saw the plight of the people and the unmet human needs brought on by hunger, disease, and poverty. *Splanchon* is often used along with *eleos* to describe mercy and compassion, but *splanchon* uniquely captures the deep human emotions of pity, mercy, and compassion as no other word does. The word denotes a person's bowels, and an adjective form of the word is used in medical terminology to describe the body's internal organs.

Given the primitive understanding of medicine at that time, human emotions were thought to be generated from within the core of a person's physical makeup, and thus the bowels became symbolic of one's deepest and most powerful feelings. We still use the concept today when we speak of a "gut feeling" about something.

Therefore, the concept is very powerful. It does not mean that Jesus felt compassion in a sympathetic, detached manner. Rather, as Jesus went through various cities and villages teaching, preaching, and "healing every sickness and disease among the people," He saw that the multitudes following Him "were weary and scattered, like sheep having no shepherd" (Matt. 9:35-36), and He felt mercy and compassion for them to the very core of His divine nature. It was a feeling of such intense compassion that He was compelled to personally act in response to the need. We must do no less.

Mercy is pouring the last drop of love on to the hardened heart, calloused soul, and defiant mind of another for whom one has deep compassion. It is the prayerful patience of a loving father awaiting the return of a wandering, prodigal son; the midnight tears of a mother shed over an erring child; the power that restores the bonds of matrimony broken by adultery; and the willingness to crawl into any gutter of shame to rescue a fallen friend. Mercy is the divine capacity to continue calling out in love against the echoes of defiance and rejection. It is the ultimate act of love, for mercy is the willingness to give up one's life and take upon oneself the sickness, suffering, and sins of another in order to save them. That is exactly what Jesus did on the cross for every redeemed Christian.

In this beatitude, Jesus introduced a challenging new dimension of mercy. He knew His covenant people must experience a fundamental change through repentance from merciless past attitudes towards others, especially sinners and those caught in the sad situations of life. No longer could God's people shun and condemn, but now they must reach out to sinners and reveal the same mercy and compassion to them they had experienced from God.

Christians are not intended to be sanctified, pious, perfectionists mercilessly imposing their standards on others. The covenant church must be a channel of redeeming love to the world through which the mercy of God flows unimpeded to all lost sinners. Thus, Jesus proclaimed the joy of a new spiritual realm in which those who show mercy to others in a positive, redemptive, loving manner will have the greatest understanding of God's mercy shown to them.

Thoughts to ponder:

1. Complete the following. I have experienced a deeper and more meaningful understanding of God's mercy by showing mercy to others in the following way:

2. Define Christian mercy in your own words based upon how you have both experienced it and shared it.

3. Could you provide examples of ways you pray to be more merciful, compassionate, and understanding toward others?

Blessed are the pure in heart, for they shall see God (Matt. 5:8).

The concept of defilement and spiritual impurity was one of the most significant issues that Jesus confronted. Cleanliness had little to do with personal hygiene, but instead defined things or people that were religiously clean or unclean before God. The laws of defilement touched every aspect of Jewish life, including how each person lived, their relationship with others, life within the home, the religious ritual of worship, and the overall attitude of Jews toward the Gentile world. In many ways, these laws defined Jews as a people and played a more important role than did the foundational laws of the Ten Commandments because of their many intricate interpretations and applications.

A thorough description of the concept of clean versus unclean would be lengthy. Simply expressed, Israel viewed herself under the covenant of law with God as being distinct, separate, religiously perfect and pure, and totally unlike any other people. In fact, the name "Pharisee," the dominant religious party, meant "the separated ones." Thus, any contact with others, or contact with the common environment around them, such as the public market, meant that one could be religiously defiled by such contact requiring immediate cleansing and purification by elaborate washing procedures.

But, how could the level of spiritual cleanliness and purity required to properly worship God be adequately defined? The possibilities are limitless. Under the Jewish law, hundreds of decisions and interpretations defined the required level of cleanliness and purity, and just as many more defined how to ceremonially cleanse something that had been previously defiled, and all had to be carefully followed.

Given the presumed serious consequences of being unclean and impure, and therefore no longer in a right relationship with God, the obvious remedy lay in a very elaborate and ceremonial system of ritualistic washing in order to rid one's self of anything that was religiously unclean. These concepts of clean versus unclean then became the subject of centuries of interpretations and arguments by rabbis, scribes and Pharisees, and even the Sanhedrin, or High Council of Israel, leading to literally volumes of minute interpretations that covered every aspect of Jewish life.

Because of the realization that one would inevitably be defiled though occasional contact with an unclean person or object, the elders of Israel developed an elaborate procedure for ritualistically washing and cleansing one's body, especially the hands, and also certain household items. The Gospel of Mark refers to these requirements in this manner:

"For the Pharisees and all the Jews do not eat unless they wash their hands in a special way, holding the tradition of the elders. When they come from the marketplace, they do not eat unless they wash. And there are many other things which they have received and hold, like the washing of cups, pitchers, copper vessels, and couches" (Mark 7:3-4).

By the time of Jesus' ministry, these ceremonial requirements had evolved into a detailed procedure in which the method and times of hand washing were specified by religious regulation and tradition, and even specified the minimum amount of water required. Usually, the hands were washed in this ritualistic manner after returning from any public outing, especially the marketplace where one would touch anything common and unclean. But the law specially required hand washing prior to eating, and some even washed between courses of food and after the meal.

Alfred Edersheim described the procedure in "The Life and Times of Jesus The Messiah:"

> "The minimum amount of water required was a measure equal to one and one-half egg shells, and it was poured on one's hands very meticulously from a ceremonially clean vessel. Water was poured on one hand and it was held with the fingers pointing upward to ensure that the water ran to the wrist, as was required. Once that hand was clean, water was then poured on the other hand. The hand that was first cleansed was clenched into a fist and used to rub the other hand. The procedure was reversed until both hands had been washed with the fists. If there was concern about the thoroughness of ceremonial cleanliness, the hands were hung downward and water was poured on the wrists and allowed to run across the hands and drip from the fingertips."

As cumbersome and odd as this may seem, for the Jews it was the only manner in which they could comprehend and experience a sense of purity and freedom from defilement that allowed them to worship God. It was the very life of their religion. But it also led to one of the greatest contradictions in the worship of God, because the law did not cleanse their hearts. However, as long as their hands were ceremonially clean when they ate bread, the thoughts of their heart did not matter.

Jesus radically transferred the source of defilement from unclean hands to one's unclean heart. He shockingly stated "But those things which proceed out of the mouth come from the heart, and they defile a man. For out of the heart proceed evil thoughts, murders, adulteries, fornications, thefts, false witness, blasphemies. These are the things which defile a man, but to eat with unwashed hands does not defile a man" (Matt. 15:17-20). That was a radical statement. Volumes of the religious law related to ceremonial cleansing of the hands and all sorts of other personal items. However, nothing in the law even remotely required a comparable cleanliness of the thoughts of one's heart.

The contrast between the obsession with physical ceremonial cleanliness and the unconcern about the impure thoughts of one's heart compelled Jesus to describe the religious leaders of Israel in a graphic manner: "Woe to you, scribes and Pharisees, hypocrites! For you are like whitewashed tombs which indeed appear beautiful outwardly, but inside are full of dead men's bones and all uncleanness" (Matt.23:27).

When Jesus said, "Blessed are the pure in heart, for they shall see God," He was speaking about the inner being of a person and the source of one's core values in life. In order for repentance to be real and transforming, Jesus set forth a new standard for those inner values, insisting upon a "purity" of heart that is free from worldly defilement and totally focused upon the true worship of God and specifically stating that it was the thoughts of one's heart that defiled him. It was a radical and shocking demand, because in stressing the purity of one's heart, Jesus did not mention the ritualistic washing of one's hands.

It is challenging to understand *kathros* (pure) in its truest sense, but it describes something which has been refined and purified to its truest natural state, or something so naturally pure that it contains not the slightest taint of impurity. It is like the presumed purity and cleanliness of the hands following a ceremonial washing with water, but now that purity applies to the thoughts and motives of the heart that has been cleansed by the blood of Jesus. King David prayed for such inner purity when he recognized the magnitude of his sins and pleaded, "Create in me a clean heart, O God" (Psalm 51:10). Such purity, especially in service to God, is indeed rare, but it is where the blessedness and joy of the kingdom of heaven are to be found.

The joyous reward of those who worship and serve God in this manner is a spiritual ability, given to them by Jesus, to "see" God in a pure and spiritually meaningful way. *Horao* (see) basically means "to stare." But whereas stare often has a negative connotation of rude behavior, it positively implies something on which one has an unbroken focus, complete attention, and unwavering interest. In effect, all of one's sensory capacities are singularly focused on what they see, and they do not take their eyes off of it regardless of the circumstances around them. Therefore, as one sees God in this manner, there is a heightened ability to clearly perceive spiritually the eternal truth of God, and in awe and adoration, humbly respond with unadulterated worship and service. That is the nature of repentance and the basis of discipleship which enables a Christian to worship God with a pure heart, for he shall clearly see the holiness of God's redeeming love for all people.

Thoughts to ponder:

1. Do you wash your hands before eating a meal? It is certainly a healthy practice and should be encouraged. Do you ever give the same attention to the purity and cleanliness of the thoughts of your heart?

2. Do you ever quietly reflect on the perfect purity of Jesus' thoughts about God, people, and life? How earnestly do you pray for His thoughts to become your thoughts?

3. When you attend church and worship God, when you pray, or when you tell others about your faith in Him, could you describe how you "see" God?

Blessed are the peacemakers, for they shall be called sons of God (Matt. 5:9).

The world in which Jesus lived was dominated by three great forces that profoundly impacted the life of all citizens—as well as the ministry of Jesus—and each offered an experience of worldly peace: the Jewish monotheistic belief in God; Greek philosophical concepts of peace and perfection; and the peace provided by the overwhelming political, economic, and military power of the Roman Empire, or the *"Pax Romana"* (the peace of Rome) that existed for roughly two hundred years within the Roman Empire from 27 B.C. to approximately 180 A.D. Into this mixture, Jesus added an additional element—Himself. Jesus specifically declared His ability to give an inner sense of spiritual peace that transcended all earthly fear and uncertainty:

"Peace I leave with you, My peace I give to you; not as the world gives do I give to you. Let not your heart be troubled, neither let it be afraid" (John 14:27). Against all of the peace provided by Roman power, Greek philosophic thought, or the Jewish hope of a messianic kingdom, Jesus offered only the inner peace that He experienced with God. His statement amazingly postures the inner spiritual peace of one man against the physical experience of peace provided by every concept of economic and military power, human achievement, and religious tradition offered by the world.

Jesus further spoke to His disciples about the events that would surround His final days on earth. In the midst of excruciating pain, disappointment, and rejection, Jesus nevertheless experienced an inner peace that transcended the physical turmoil around Him, and He directly attributed that to God's unbroken presence with Him:

"Indeed the hour is coming, yes, and has now come, that you will be scattered, each to his own, and will leave Me alone. And yet I am not alone, because the Father is with Me. These things I have spoken to you, that in Me you may have peace. In the world you will have tribulation; but be of good cheer, I have overcome the world" (John 16:32-33).

No other statement in history compares with Jesus' statement, either in its importance to every Christian or to the world as a whole. If one can experience complete peace with God, then he can know peace within himself, and if he is at peace with himself, then he can be at peace with his neighbors, and if he is at peace with his neighbors, then there can finally be peace on earth and good will among men.

But Jesus did not speak of just His own peace. Rather, He commissioned His disciples as "peacemakers" themselves. The only time that *eirenopoios* (peacemaker) is used in the New Testament is in this beatitude, for the word alone describes the ultimate priestly work of Jesus and the ongoing ministry of those who follow Him. Jesus is the ultimate fulfillment of the Old Testament peace offering, and He alone reconciles believers to God and allows them to enter into God's peace through faith in Him and thereby experience eternal, unbroken communion with God. Spiritual peace is a Christian's experience when all spiritual strife and separation from God have been eliminated, and he is redeemed and restored to an unbroken covenant relationship with God, thus allowing Jesus' peace to become his own.

But, how did Jesus make peace so that His disciples can then be peacemakers also? Out of the maelstrom of spiritual divisiveness, Jesus brought all people to the foot of His cross through personal faith in the finality of His redemptive work for them. Henceforth, each believer would find peace with God only through faith in the final peace offering of Jesus on the cross. For all would find equality in the cross, all would need forgiveness of sin, all would enter the kingdom of heaven on the same basis, all would receive the same outpouring of divine love and grace, none would have any claim of spiritual superiority over the other, and all mankind could experience peace with one another, for the spiritual divisions and distinctions separating them had been removed by faith in Jesus.

The work of a peacemaker is an intensely personal experience. Faithfully, it is there, at the foot of His cross, that I and my Christian brothers and sisters, from all social and economic backgrounds and of every race, color, and creed, gather in a unique bond of covenant love. Amazingly, it is there, at the foot of His cross, that one finds that the atoning blood of Jesus mercifully falls on all of us, cleansing us from our sins, and that God's love, mercy, and grace have been equally and abundantly poured out on all of us, for none is better or worse than the other, because we all have sinned and fallen short of the glory of God. Gratefully, it is there, at the foot of His cross, that we discover that we all have inherited equal portions of the heavenly kingdom graciously given to us by our Father in heaven, for none of us have been treated with any greater favor or love than others. Joyously, it is there, at the foot of His cross, that I realize that my brothers and sisters and I are divinely adopted as children of God and that there is no distinction or division among us. Thankfully, it is there, at the foot of His cross, with tears of praise flowing, that I find peace both with God and with my brothers and sisters in Christ. And, humbly, it is there, at the foot of His cross, that I commit my life to His redeeming work and experience the blessed joy of a peacemaker.

The Apostle Paul stated that those who believe in Jesus through faith are adopted by God and, "…as many as are led by the Spirit, these are sons of God" (Rom. 8:14-16). Thus, anyone referred to as a "son of God" understands his direct relationship with God, realizes that his very life comes from Him, models himself in His image, commits his life to the will and work of his heavenly Father, and experiences the peace of his Father. Jesus is the one Son of God who truly lived this relationship, but He gives His peace to all His disciples who are sons of God like Him.

Thoughts to ponder:

1. Complete the following statement: My personal Christian ministry as a peacemaker involves the following…

2. When I pray for peace on earth, am I thinking mostly of political, military, and economic peace, such as the absence of war, or am I praying for worldwide spiritual peace with God through faith in Christ?

3. How has your faith in Jesus brought you a spiritual peace that is greater than all other sources of peace and security you seek in the world?

Blessed are those who are persecuted for righteousness sake, for theirs is the kingdom of heaven (Matt. 5:10).

Jesus was a true idealist in many ways, but He was also a pragmatic realist who knew from the beginning of His ministry that the spiritual ideals He proclaimed would not be widely received. He further knew that the principles of faith, love, and mercy which He taught, combined with total devotion and consecration to God, would not be broadly accepted at any time, either by the religious leadership in Israel or by the world as a whole. Thus, Jesus realistically prepared Himself and His disciples to encounter serious opposition, even while faithfully striving to instill those new principles of righteousness in the heart of God's covenant people.

This beatitude is not solely about the experience of having bad things said or done because of one's Christian faith. In a broader sense, it is about the clash of two cultures borne out of two entirely different concepts of life. The beatitude simply and succinctly describes the effect that the physical, economic, and social forces of the world will have upon those who have entered the spiritual kingdom of heaven by faith. It is Jesus' frank assessment of the consequences of consecration.

The fundamental truth of the beatitude is not only how the world will react to the godly life of a Christian, but more importantly how the Christian will respond to the pressure of living this new life in a world—and even among family and friends—which may neither understand nor appreciate one's spiritual values. The common experience of many is that pressure will come from different sources, and in diverse ways, seeking to diminish one's Christian life

Intense emotional pressure is what Jesus envisioned when He realistically warned His disciples that "in the world you will have tribulation" (John 16:33). Jesus truthfully told His disciples that persecution and tribulation would be their ongoing experience as they lived for Him, and it would come in all forms and degrees of intensity. Rather than solely describing some future experience of torture, the concept of tribulation also denotes crushing emotional and spiritual pressure caused by circumstances in everyday Christian life that produce frustration and distress.

Not every Christian undergoes such turmoil, and many live a peaceful life free from any adverse pressure. On the other hand, Christianity is not the panacea for happiness that some make it out to be. Truly, it is a life filled with spiritual joy and thanksgiving to God for one's salvation and the inner spiritual peace given by Jesus. But, if one is consistently true to his faith in Jesus and strives never to compromise his consecration to God, there will inevitably be moments, whether great or small in significance, in which he will encounter resistance and pressure to compromise which can take many painful and harmful forms.

Interestingly, if the beatitudes were compiled into a description of a single personality and life, that individual would be as different from a carnal, worldly oriented person as day is from night. Taken as a whole, the beatitudes describe one who has a sense of personal spiritual poverty and humility before God; possesses a broken and contrite heart produced by deep, heartfelt grief over the consequences of his own personal transgression of God's holiness; has a resolute determination to use all of his talents and abilities to glorify God through personal submission to Jesus as Lord; experiences a deep spiritual hunger and thirst for the fullness of God's righteousness through faith in Christ that supersedes the desire for any other thing; reveals a true sense of mercy and compassion for others that compels one to become personally involved in alleviating human suffering and to compassionately care for sinners rather than shunning them; is driven by a passion to serve and glorify God in every aspect of his life, without the slightest desire for personal glory, gain, or accolade; and sincerely desires to share the gospel and peace of Jesus Christ with others, so they too may experience a heavenly peace within their earthly circumstances that comes only through faith in Jesus.

The Beatitudes are not separate guidelines for spiritual happiness. They do not describe cafeteria-style Christianity in which you are free to select the ones you like best and ignore the rest. They must be considered as a whole; none take priority over the others. These interrelated spiritual concepts describe the committed life of one who has chosen to live diametrically opposite to those obsessed with worldly pursuits.

The persecution that Jesus described occurs, in some form or fashion, as a Christian lives this repentant life in the midst of an ungodly world increasingly focused on personal greed and gratification. It will be different for each Christian, but situations will develop in which one is taunted, reviled, upbraided, and insulted for his godly beliefs. Scathing remarks questioning his spiritual motives, derogatory comments belittling his beliefs, and denunciation of positions he takes become routine experiences.

Persecution describes one's reaction and interestingly means "to flee." It portrays someone being under such pressure that escaping to a safer and less stressful environment appears to be the only recourse. Persecution, therefore, is not limited to torture or imprisonment, but may include situations where the pressure that one experiences from being a faithful servant becomes so intense that he simply wants to get away. Every true Christian either has been or will be in a situation of that nature.

However, Jesus offered His followers a way to turn tribulation and persecution into triumph. He told them to "rejoice and be exceedingly glad" (Matt. 5:12) when they encountered such trials and difficulties. The phrase "exceedingly glad" describes an experience of joy so intense that it causes one to dance around, or more specifically, to "jump for joy" out of sheer happiness. But that isn't as easy to do as it sounds. It's hard to jump for joy when you feel as if the weight of the world is on your shoulders.

Therefore, the disciples of Jesus must be prepared to experience every conceivable thing that will oppose, diminish, counteract, and reduce the impact of their witness for Christ. It is not limited to some future experience of torture and turmoil; rather, it is just everyday life for the truly committed Christian who strives to live a godly life in an ungodly world.

Thankfully, Jesus proclaimed a divine reward for His faithful servants that transcends the evil of this world when He said, "for theirs is the kingdom of heaven." Jesus promised those who experience persecution and tribulation from living righteously for Him on earth will be blessed with the fullest realization of the peace, beauty, and truth of the heavenly realm. And for that, we can indeed be exceedingly glad.

Thoughts to ponder:

1. Have you ever rejoiced in the midst of spiritual turmoil knowing that the pain you were experiencing was for "righteousness" sake?

2. Could you describe an instance where you felt so alone and rejected because of your Christian beliefs that you simply wanted to get away from the situation and go somewhere else?

3. Have you ever looked at the Beatitudes as a collective description of a dedicated Christian and asked yourself, "Does this describe me?"

Comfort

My cat made me consider a biblical truth I had never fully realized. While looking at him resting his head in an odd position, for some reason I began thinking about the meaning of comfort, and not just physical comfort, but rather the nature of spiritual comfort mentioned numerous times in the Bible.

This might interest you, just as it did me. Jesus gives numerous spiritual blessings to Christians that are a part of our salvation experience, such as rest, peace, and joy. But the Gospels do not state that Jesus gives us "comfort." Jesus obviously stated that those who mourn will be comforted, but He didn't specify in the beatitude the source of that comfort.

Granting spiritual comfort to believers is the primary work of the Holy Spirit, and He does it in a unique way. Jesus said the Holy Spirit would take all things that are given to Jesus by the Father and "declare" them to us. The best way to understand the meaning of "declare" is to think of some statement, blessing, or experience that is final, full, and complete. It is the work of making something so fully clear and understandable that all doubt is removed and nothing further is needed to grasp its meaning.

If the Holy Spirit fully declares the comfort of God to us, that would make Him our personal "Comforter," wouldn't it? And that is precisely how Jesus described Him: "But the Comforter, who is the Holy Spirit, whom the Father will send in my name...." His work is described early in the Old Testament. Isaiah the prophet exclaimed, "Comfort, comfort my people." But what does that mean? Basically, it describes the tenderness and mercy of God, who is so moved by divine pity and compassion over our human plight, that He personally takes our struggles upon Himself, lifts those burdens from us, and becomes our Comforter.

We pray to God for all kinds of things, and we ask Jesus for forgiveness and many other blessings. However, we don't often pray for the Holy Spirit to "declare" the comfort of God both in our life and through our life. Oh, but what a difference it would make if we did.

Honestly, I am sickened by the rancor and bitterness that people, including Christians, spread on social media. I am disillusioned by the division amongst us. Why can't we pray for comfort for others instead? Are "thoughts and prayers" for victims of senseless violence and tragic storms all we can do? Can we not do more to bring comfort to them?

Rather than condemning our political leadership with vile, derogatory statements, can we not pray for God's comfort to be granted to them? Can we not change our bitter rhetoric and pray for our president, as God's word tells us to do, rather than denounce him? It takes no more effort to pray for someone than to curse them.

Can we, as Christians, please get it out of our head and mind that Easter is all about colored eggs and bunny rabbits, and instead finally understand that Easter and the resurrection of Jesus is when the unrestrainable power of the Holy Spirit began to take "all things" of Christ and fully declare them to us.

When we as individuals and a nation finally get that through our thick skull, the experience of Easter will move from our head to our heart, and then we shall be comforted.

The Red Sea Place in Your Life

It was a moment I will never forget. It seemed like life was nothing but one big demand...the demands of caring for elderly, sick parents, the expectations and demands of church members, the demands of hospital executives and impatient doctors, and the physical and financial demands of life in general. To say the emotional and spiritual outflow far exceeded the inflow is an understatement. I was drained, demoralized, and virtually defeated.

I retreated to the quiet, reverential atmosphere of the hospital chapel, and I sat there considering the options before me. I asked God for help. In a matter of moments, my attention was drawn to a small plaque on the wall, and I walked to it and read it:

> "When you come to the Red Sea place in your life, when in spite of all you can do, there is no way round, there is no way back, there is no other way but through, then know God with a soul serene, and the dark and the storms are gone. God stills the wind, God stills the waves, God says to your soul, 'Go On! Go On! Go On!'"

I was stunned and overwhelmed by the message divinely spoken to me through those words. I copied it down, and a church member later made it into a needlepoint for me. I cherish it and have kept it hanging on my wall for the last thirty years.

We all face a Red Sea place in our life at times. But there's no going back to the joy of yesterday, there's no going around the pain and despair of today, and the only way to go is through and pray for a better tomorrow. One moment at a time...one step at a time...one day at a time. It is a journey of hope that must be walked down a tear-stained path, and it can be dark and lonely, but it must be made. We have no choice.

The voice of God—the same God to whom we painfully cry out "Why?"— quietly whispers to our troubled soul, "Go On, Go On, Go On. I will get you to the other side of disaster and despair." And on the other side, you will look back and wonder how you made it, and you will find your answer: "God brought me through it."

Rest

Maybe it's just the effects of advancing age and a weakening heart, but rest has become vitally important to me. Years ago, when I had the energy to toot my whistle a bit louder than I can now, I commuted to Jackson every day and worked at Baptist Medical Center, served as pastor of a growing church, and tended a small farm. To borrow the scriptural phrase, at times I was "weary and heavy laden," but there was little time to rest. Sensing my fatigue, a wise, observant, and compassionate older lady quietly slipped a note into my hand one Sunday after the church service that read:

"If you put your nose to the grindstone rough, and you hold it there long enough, you'll soon forget the sounds of spring and brooks that babble and birds that sing. And of these three things your life will be composed: you, the stone, and your ground off nose." "Get some rest," she added. I've thought about her comment many times over the years, both from a physical and a spiritual standpoint.

Have you ever considered that Easter is actually about rest? That might surprise some of you, so let me explain.

Rest is an ancient biblical concept dating back to creation, at the conclusion of which God "rested." But God wasn't physically fatigued and needed to sink into a heavenly recliner and sip on a Gatorade, as I would be.

Rather, the meaning of "rest" is based on the idea of completion of a work, and that work is so perfect that nothing more can be done. When the divine work of creation was totally finished, God ceased His efforts, and thus He "rested."

The same can be said about the divine work of redemption. When Jesus said "It is finished" from the cross, He bowed His head and died, and He entered into His rest. There was nothing more that He could do to atone for our sins. Jesus had said, "Come to Me, all you who labor and are heavy laden, and I will give you rest." Jesus had also earlier prayed in the Garden of Gethsemane, "I have finished the work which You gave Me to do." He would now give the work of bestowing His rest and peace on believers to the Holy Spirit. He could not give us His rest unless He knew that level of divine rest personally. He had finished His work.

"Rest" results from ceasing personal effort and labor. Hebrews 4:9-10 states, "There remains therefore a rest for the people of God." But it isn't just a day of rest, as we sometimes refer to Sunday, but rather a life- transforming spiritual experience of rest. "For he who has entered His rest has himself also ceased from his works as God did from His." Think about that: When we enter into Jesus' rest, we cease our wearisome labor, and we rest just as God did. We experience the meaning of a Sabbath rest.

For each of you personally, Easter means that Jesus has finished the work of your redemption. There's nothing more you can do except believe in faith in the sufficiency of His work and the grace of God that bestows it upon you. You can cease all your efforts of self-righteous goodness and your belief that your works earn God's favor. You can lift your nose from the grindstone of religious ritual that leaves you more spiritually drained than inspired. You can cease being afraid of God and instead experience the boundless love of your heavenly Father. You can cease fearing the future and rejoice in the truth that "morning by morning, new mercies I see."

You can look at the cross and the empty tomb of Jesus and quietly say to yourself, "My redemption is finished. My salvation is certain. My future is secure. I can cease my work and my worry. I can rest."

It Wasn't Much, but it was Enough

My grandfather was a master of "make-do." He didn't have many earthly possessions, so he learned to make do both with what he had and what he could make. Raising a family on a worn-out South Mississippi cotton farm in the terrible economic strain of the Great Depression will cause that, I suppose.

Grandpa would take a broken straight-back chair and make a new seat for it from whatever he had available, and sometimes he got rather creative. He cut strips of tree bark and created a basket-weave bottom for one chair, and he used cow hide for another. There was also one in which he used strips of rubber inner tube from a car tire to weave together a bottom. Nearly a century later, they're still strong and usable.

He also would cut small, forked tree branches and make wall hangers to use in the house and barn. They held both clothes and mule harness equally well. It wasn't much, but it was enough, and it would make do.

Several years ago, I was driving home one night down a dark, lonely highway, and my thoughts were mentally going in all directions. I turned on the car radio and was immediately captivated by the beautiful, deep voice of an old black preacher coming from somewhere in the heartland of America. His sermon had a recurring line that he used with amazing effectiveness and power: "It wasn't much, but it was enough."

He verbally carried me through the Bible with eloquence that drew my wandering thoughts to his words like a magnet. He described things that would seem to be so insignificant, such as the small pitch-lined basket in which baby Moses floated and the little pebbles in David's slingshot. After a couple of seconds of silent pause, he would say, "It wasn't much, but it was enough."

He then brought me to the crucifixion and resurrection of Jesus. This old country preacher had me mentally feeling the weight and roughness of the cross and holding the sharp, rusty nails in my hand. I saw the little stone outcropping called Golgotha and watched in horror as the cross was lifted up. And then he said, "It wasn't much, but it was enough."

This godly servant then took me inside the cool, rock tomb in which Jesus' body was placed. With increasing Holy Spirit passion known only to a true, God-called preacher, he then verbally rolled back the stone with verbal eloquence and power that I had never heard. And then he paused: "It wasn't much, but it was enough." By then, tears were streaming down my face.

As we prepare to celebrate Easter, we should be reminded that, by the world's standards, an old wooden cross and an empty stone tomb aren't much, but in the hands of God, they are enough, and they'll make do.

I'm Too Old to be This Cold

Merle Haggard had a great country song entitled, "If We Make it Through December," and the opening line was "If we make it through December, everything's going to be alright I know," and the closing line is "If we make it through December we'll be fine." I feel the same way about March.

All the beds of red amaryllis that were in beautiful full bloom now look like red-topped popsicles right out of the freezer. The knockout roses look like they've been knocked out, and I'm afraid to look at blueberry bushes and peach trees. I don't have any recipes for frozen, marble-size peaches.

But I do find things to be thankful for in this cold. I'm thankful that I'm not trying to heat this house with three little fireplaces where most of the heat goes up the chimney, or trying to start a fire in the wood-burning stove and roll out a pan of hog-lard biscuits. I'm glad I don't have to go to the cold barn and milk a cow so I can have milk—and hope she doesn't set her dirty hoof in the milk bucket. I'm glad I don't have to cut firewood today with a dull crosscut saw, and I'm glad I don't have to build a fire around a black washpot out in the yard to wash clothes and hang them on the fence and hope they dry in the cold wind. I'm thankful I don't have to heat bath water on the stove, pour it in a tub, and take a bath on the back porch. I'm thankful I don't have to walk out across the backyard unbuckling my overalls to spend a few minutes sitting in a freezing cold outhouse, while looking through a Sears catalog. But my family did all that while living in this century-old house. When I think of them, my reasons to complain seem to diminish.

It may be cold outside, but I'm so thankful for a warm house, plenty of food, modern conveniences, gas and electric heat, and no cows to milk. The Good Lord has bountifully blessed us, and we should thank Him every day for the comforts of home.

The flowers will grow back, the grass will get green again, and the sun will soon warm us up. Tomorrow the birds will be joyously chirping their songs of Spring once more. To paraphrase ole Merle, "...if we can make it through March, we'll be fine."

Putting Your Hand to the Plow

Once you have smelled plowed dirt, the desire to till and stir good soil becomes locked into your psyche. Maybe it's some subconscious mental reversion to our ancient ancestral days when we stopped being hunters and became planters. I don't know.

I don't farm anymore, but there were days in my past where I found great satisfaction in hooking a disk to my John Deere and watching the soil turn up behind me. The combination of spring warmth, sunshine, fresh air, the smell of freshly plowed soil, and the slight diesel smell from the tractor's exhaust fumes all made for simple, down-home, rural happiness.

I often watch videos of tractors plowing on large farms, and I'm totally amazed at their size, often covering several feet in width. But for Grandpa Voss, and other farmers of his generation, it was not that way. I look at the assortment of breaking plows and the middle buster, and I am shocked to realize that these old implements only plowed about ten inches in width, if that much. I can't imagine the tiresome, back-breaking toil of plowing up several acres following a mule and taking off only ten inches of soil each time.

That was just the initial plowing. Then came disking, harrowing, and planting, all following the same tired mule. The Good Lord only knows how often "gee" (go right) or "haw" (go left) was yelled at poor ole Sam and Ida. I marvel at the strength and perseverance of both man and beast. I simply don't know how they did it, but they did.

Operating a plow was no easy task and required a fair amount of skill learned from experience and practice. One pushed down on the handles to make it plow shallower or lifted them up to go deeper, and pushing the plow handles left or right turned the plow—all while walking in uneven, plowed ground behind a stubborn mule that had no desire to be yelled at or tapped on its rump with the reins.

A straight furrow could only be plowed by looking straight ahead because the plow went in the wrong direction the minute you looked back at where you'd been. When you looked behind, a furrow could oftentimes end up very crooked and unsightly, and no good plowman wanted that.

That is why Jesus used this simple example from everyday life to make one of His most powerful statements about the level of our spiritual commitment: "No one, having put his hand to the plow, and looking back, is fit for the kingdom of God." That is such a simple illustration, and yet so powerful. I've been teaching and preaching the gospel for nearly fifty years, and it is my firm belief that the great tragedy confronting both America and the church is the lack of true commitment to Christ from professing Christians. More time is spent on remembering the sins of yesterday than seeking the heavenly kingdom's spiritual sanctification of today and tomorrow. You see and hear it both in their talk and in their walk.

If ever there was a need for a true spiritual revival and awakening in this country, it is now. It can begin with each of us. When you put your hand on the plow handle of commitment to Christ, never look back!

Two Cats Named Chaos and Confusion

It's amazing how two half-grown kittens can make a grown man yell out words not found in your Sunday School Quarterly, but it's true. If there's such a thing as a cat being demon possessed, I have two that got an extra helping of satanic mischief. If Jesus could cast demons into a herd of swine and make them run off a cliff and into the sea, surely, He could touch these two little hellions and transform them into nice little kitties, before they drive me off a cliff—assuming I could find one in Lamar County. Maybe driving me up a tall loblolly pine tree would be more workable.

It all began with such good intentions. The kittens were thrown out in Coaltown Cemetery by some heartless oaf, and I ended up giving them a home that saved their lives. Just what every animal-loving person with a tender heart should do, right? And you'd think such a kind gesture would be rewarded, wouldn't you? But, au contraire, gratitude isn't their attitude.

Does a cat have a climbing gear? Indeed, they do, and it is one of their earliest developed physical features. Rather than looking at the floor where they can learn to walk and run better, these two stroll around with their heads in the air looking for something to climb, and I am likely to find them anywhere, such as on top of bookcases, atop the refrigerator, or swinging from a lamp shade. Never leave a cabinet door open in front of them, or you will be up in the cabinet trying to pull them out of the pots and pans. How about finding one of them sitting in the refrigerator when the door got accidentally shut on it.

It's hard to pinpoint when our relationship turned sour. But maybe if I share a few instances of midnight madness, you can get a better understanding of why I gave them their well-deserved names. Let's begin with the broken decorative plate incident. I've had a plate painted with a beautiful country scene for about thirty years. It was sitting on a stand on my roll top desk, and I noticed one of the cats walking on the top of the desk near the plate. "Get down!" I yelled. Did satanic Sally quietly remove herself from the desk? Oh no, the opposite happened. She did a swan dive straight onto the plate and knocked it on to the floor, breaking it into about ten pieces. This was followed by a mad chase around the room with me swinging my Dollar General discount broom at her. When she stopped under a chair and looked at me with that evil look on her face, I threw the broom at her and promptly broke the head off the broom—even before I could sweep up the broken plate. More harsh words fell upon kitty's tender ears.

How about the broken Christmas gift? My niece gave me a beautiful mug many years ago containing the name and colors of my favorite school. Chaos and Confusion apparently have become Bulldog fans, so they concocted a scheme to rid themselves of the Ole Miss reminder and also send their old master further into the throes of mindless anger. In the middle of the night, they jumped on top of a bookcase and pushed the mug and two pictures of my great-grandparents off and broke the mug followed by more midnight yelling and cats running for cover.

How about them hiding my black Cross ballpoint pen that I've had for years? Yes, indeed, they can do that. The pen was in my checkbook on my kitchen bar, but those little hellish heifers removed the pen and pushed it across the bar onto the floor. That was just the beginning. They then pushed it across the kitchen floor and made it drop down behind a carpeted step going down into the den—but there was more. They then figured out how to push the pen up under the edge of the step where it could not be seen. So, I looked and looked, and just on a wild hunch, I pushed the step aside and there was my pen. You have to be an evil genius to devise such a plan.

But I've saved the best for last. I have a few chickens here, and I put the eggs in a wooden tray on my kitchen counter against the far wall. Chaos and Confusion plotted the most wicked scheme to light this old man up, and they succeeded. During the night, they jumped on the cabinet and got into the egg tray. I can just hear them now, "What if we roll these eggs off into the floor and watch that old man step in the broken eggs when he stumbles in here for coffee in the morning?" "Great Idea!" they no doubt meowed to each other, and so they did.

How two cats can push three eggs out of a tray and across a cabinet top and roll them into the floor where they shattered is beyond me, but they did. And their plan worked perfectly. Can you picture me stepping barefoot into three broken eggs and then hopping around the kitchen trying to wipe eggs off my foot, while glancing up and seeing two cats sitting on top of the refrigerator enjoying every moment of the show? I think there is probably some community standard code that prevents me from sharing what I said to these two little demons.

There's more, but if I typed it all, I'd have to go take a blood pressure pill. So what do they do when they know they have pushed me to the brink? They cuddle up in my lap with such innocence that it cuts through the anger and brings out forgiveness. And we start the process all over again.

If I were to wax philosophic about the schemes of these cats, I'd have to say that maybe God sees the chaos and confusion in our own life, and He really isn't happy with us at times, either. But His longsuffering with us, and His compassion, always produces understanding of our human nature and His forgiveness of our twisted ways results, if we truly and sincerely confess our evil doings to Him. I'm just very thankful that my Heavenly Father hasn't thrown His broom at me yet.

Righteousness Exalts a Nation

I'm fascinated with the power of words. I enjoy exploring their origin and original meaning and how we have adapted them into the vocabulary of our culture. I want to share my thoughts with you about three words.

Bedlam is an interesting word with which to begin. We use it to describe chaos, confusion, and uncontrolled disruption. Interestingly, Bedlam was the name of the oldest mental institution in London, existing several hundred years ago. Because of the actions of patients, and how those in charge reacted to them, Bedlam became synonymous with a place of uncontrolled confusion and disruption.

Bedlam opened a new facility last night in Washington, and we know it as the House of Representatives. I watched in disbelief and dismay as those who were elected through the trust of ordinary Americans abandoned restraint and reason and gutlessly groveled in the gutter of political chicanery to grasp power over others. Men and women of presumed honor cast aside the cloak of decency and dignity and fought, cursed, cajoled, and threatened each other like crazed drunks intoxicated by the prize of power—power to pass laws that will possibly create more bedlam in America.

I have been a student of law, American government, and politics since my early years of watching John Kennedy, Richard Nixon, and Lyndon Johnson. I should have learned then that politics was as full of smelly deals as the dairy barnyard from which I longed to escape was full of …well, you get my point. Friday night only reinforced my opinion.

Righteousness is a second interesting word. It is directly associated with actions and attitudes that God highly favors. Basically, it is how God wishes for people to treat each other—with respect, decency, compassion, and deeply caring about the needs of one another. It is the basis on which God pours out His favor on a nation and blesses them.

Exalt is the third word. The wise writer of Proverbs says that God finds favor with a righteous nation and lifts them up as a symbol for all others to see and follow. That nation becomes a model for all other people to emulate. Exalting a righteous people is "well-pleasing" to God.

But the opposite is bedlam. The opposite is being a people crazed by power and consumed with fighting, fussing, and fisticuffs in the highest and most cherished chambers of democratic government. Bedlam is principles of conscience sacrificed at midnight on the tarnished altar of greed; souls being sold to the devil of deception for one more vote; and men and women ripping off their bright robes of personal restraint, dignity, and decorum and willingly throwing themselves on the naked harlot's bed of shame for one more endorsement of their crooked schemes.

Friday night saddened me as deeply as anything ever has in my sixty years of watching our national leaders in action. Friday night, about midnight, I came to a deeper understanding of the original meaning of bedlam.

America has a choice. We can continue the political bedlam and madness, and the craziness will only worsen. Or, each of us can return in our own belief system to that which God favors and which He will bless and exalt as a model of democratic government for all the world to see—"One nation under God with liberty and justice for all."

America's future is in our hands. May God help us.

Dear Daddy: A Different Kind of Father's Day Poem

Sunday is Father's Day, and it's a special day for many. My father was never close to his three sons, and my parents' divorce when I was ten deeply impacted me. Years ago, I drove past his house one day as I was going to pay my utility bill, and he was standing in his yard. I simply said to myself, "How are you today, dear daddy?" Those words flipped a switch, and more words quickly began flowing. You might find this hard to believe, but I wrote most of this sitting in the REA parking lot in Purvis, using every piece of scrap paper I could find in my truck. It does not reflect any circumstances of my childhood; it's just a poem. But for any fathers who think that your indifference and absence in your child's life does not matter, you are so very wrong. Your absence will impact them for life. Trust me.

"Dear Daddy"

With pen in hand,
I thought of the man
and wondered just what I would say.
For I saw his name in the paper today
that tomorrow they would lay him away.

It had been twenty years
and a river of tears
since I last heard him call out my name.
And day after day, since he went away,
I wondered if I was to blame.

But I wanted some way
that finally I could say
what I felt in my sad, hurting soul,
as I looked at the pictures of daddy and me
and the little-boy memories they hold.

It was late in the night
that I decided to write
what my life without him had been
and put it in the hand of this cold, distant man,
for I would never see him again.

"Dear Daddy, why did you leave,
why couldn't you stay?
You left without saying goodbye,
and I'm trying to be strong, but I feel so alone,
and at night I try not to cry."

I remembered just then,
that when I was ten,
I had written him these very same lines,
and I waited each day, to hear what he would say,
but finally just gave up in time.

Was it something I did,
or something I said,
that caused you some heart-breaking pain?
If only I knew, then I'd promise you
never to do that again.

When I was fifteen,
if only you'd seen
me driving that ole GMC.
Mama taught me her best, and I passed that ole test,
but I wish you had been there with me.

I hunted and fished,
but oh how I wished
for you to teach me all that you knew.
And out there alone, I imagined you home,
just me, mama, and you.

When I was sixteen,
tall, hungry, and lean,
I thought I had become my own man.
But you'll never know how I missed you so
and the touch of my daddy's strong hand.

I learned how to shave,
and I tried to be brave,
and be someone that would make you so proud.
I had a job on Saturday, and gave mama my pay
and I never was in the wrong crowd.

I had a hound dog named Jake
that I'd often take
down the lane to the ole swimming hole.
We'd splash and we'd play,
but there came the sad day
when ole Jake got too sick and too old.

And as I walked away
from where I buried him that day,
neath the white oak with the stream running by,
it was so hard to do, but I remembered how you,
used to tell me that big boys don't cry.

Daddy, why did you leave,
why couldn't you stay?
You left without saying goodbye.
I'm trying to be strong, but I feel so alone,
and at night I try not to cry.

When I was eighteen,
unknowing and green,
I had my first taste of true love.
She was pretty and sweet, and swept me right off my feet,
like an angel sent down from above.

But I was just a kid,
and the stupid thing that I did
put an end to my hopes and plans.
For after a while, she was carrying our child,
and I had to start being a man.

It wasn't too long
before the love was all gone
and our life became an everyday hell.
Finally, one day I just walked away,
for I guess you had taught me too well.

I saw him one day,
in his front yard at play,
and I slowed as he raised up his head.
I stopped to say hi, and he looked me straight in the eye,
and here's what my little boy said:

"Daddy, why did you leave,
why couldn't you stay?
You left without saying goodbye.
I'm trying to be strong, but I feel so alone,
and at night I try not to cry."

Maybe some way,
on some distant day,
I'll understand it as my life unfolds.
But through bitter tears, I think only of the years
and the heart-breaking memories they hold.

I guess I waited too long,
after you were gone,
to tell you of my life-long prayer:
that somehow you'd have cared, and a life we'd have shared,
just me, mama, and you.

Silently he lay
in his casket so gray,
and I didn't know just how I'd feel,
when I took hold of the hand of this cold, lifeless man,
as the chapel bells began softly to peel.

My words were few,
but somehow I knew,
that I had to say this one last time:
"It's time for me to go, but I just wanted you to know,
dear Daddy, I have always loved you."

Then I took the note,
the one that I wrote,
that told him of my hopes and fears,
and I put it in the hand of this stone-cold man,
and quietly asked him the same thing I'd asked him for years:

"Daddy, why did you leave,
why couldn't you say?
You left without saying goodbye.
I'm trying to be strong, but I feel so alone,
and tonight I'll try not to cry.

Daddy, why did you leave…?"

A Country Boy's View of Democracy

We will soon be celebrating the Fourth of July, and the taste of barbeque, watermelon, and homemade ice cream is already dancing around in my mind. The Fourth of July has long held special meaning to me because I am captivated by the power of the Declaration of Independence and the courage of those who signed it. Several provisions of the Declaration are especially significant to me.

You might be interested in something I wrote fifty-eight years ago as a seventeen-year-old student at Purvis High School as my entry in a writing contest about American government. I've kept it in a file for these past decades. Hopefully, the writing quality has improved over the years, but the content still rings true.

"What Democracy Means to Me"

Democracy is the form of government by which we here in America are governed. However, if we consider it only in the literal sense, we miss out on the true meaning of democracy. Why does it work? What makes it the greatest form of government ever conceived by the minds of mortal men? Why should you and I, as citizens, be willing to sacrifice our lives, our fortunes, and our sacred honor for this form of government? When we can answer these questions, then—and only then—have we discovered the true meaning of democracy.

Why does democracy work? If any form of government is to be successful, the wishes and desires of the people must be incorporated in it. Democracy has this quality. Democracy has achieved its success through the principle of election of officials by the people, thus keeping the influence of the people on the government to a maximum and the influence of the government on the people to a minimum.

How has democracy achieved its greatness? Why is it the most envied form of government on earth? The greatness of a government is achieved through the interest of the people in it and the efforts they put forth to perpetuate its greatness. Democracy has this quality. In American history we have witnessed an almost unbelievable miracle. The fact that people of various races, creeds, and colors have come together and formed a bond of government and have worked side by side for the common interest of the government is miraculous. And through this form of government, people have been able to achieve anything their physical and mental abilities might provide for them.

Why should we be ready to sacrifice our all for our democratic way of life? If there is to be one main item singled out as being the most important thing that has been instilled in the minds of the American people, this item would be pride. For in the last 189 years, we have accumulated much to be proud of. When a man is proud enough of his country and of his way of life, and is concerned enough over the fact that these things must be conserved for the benefit of his posterity that he is willing to sacrifice his life, then he is within the highest traditions of the American way of life and of democracy.

These preceding statements represent the true meaning of democracy to me. It is not just a form of government, but rather a flexible, working agreement between the people in which provisions are made for the formation of a governing body, and other requirements necessary for the proper functioning of a country, and through this agreement combining the ideas of many into one.

And now the enormous task of preserving democracy is about to fall upon the shoulders of our generation. To prepare ourselves for this responsibility, we must develop good qualities of citizenship. This can be achieved by applying ourselves to the extent of our ability in our school work, because a successful citizen is a knowledgeable citizen.

We must adopt for ourselves a strong moral code and abide by its provisions. We must not be afraid to do what we know is right. We must be individualistic and know the extent to which we can afford to be influenced by others.

We must learn to be responsible and trustworthy. For if we cannot meet these requirements, then we shall only be a social handicap to our community.

We must actively participate in local governmental and community affairs. The more interest we have in democracy and the more we strive to improve it, the stronger it will get, thereby benefitting everyone.

By doing these things and by maintaining an undying faith if the infinite power of Almighty God, the light of American democracy will not flicker or fail.

I didn't win the contest, but it would have been helpful if I had. I think the prize was twenty-five dollars, and, in 1965, mama could have bought groceries for a week from Otis and Ruby Sue's store with that. Times have changed.

Finding Your Father on a Lonely Dirt Road

I want you to go with me in your heart and mind to a place you may not have been before, but until you go there, you will not truly appreciate the power and divine holiness of a father's godly love. The parable of the prodigal son covers a broad period of time, but it's life-transforming spiritual impact covers a time span of less than five minutes. It occurs along a dusty road outside an unnamed city and involves only two people, a father and his long-lost son. Quietly and reverently go there with me in your imagination so that you can personally experience what happened.

The young man is walking slowly and hesitatingly, his head bowed and his shoulders stooped, as if he is physically forcing his hot, dusty feet to take each step. He is walking toward his father's house, and it is a journey he does not want to make...a journey he never intended to make in the earlier days of his rebellious youth when he seemed so certain about the defiant course he had chosen in life.

But his circumstances had radically changed for the worse, and he found himself emotionally consumed by nightmarish despair he never envisioned. He had wasted the inheritance demanded from his father, he had abandoned his native land and moved to a foreign country, and he became so desperate and hungry that he ate the food of unclean swine. Through his foolishness and extravagant living, he had destroyed his relationship with his father, his country, and his God.

Now he was a broken young man slowly walking toward the fatal fate that awaited him. He knew that his father had the legal right and authority to stone him to death, and that's what he expected. But he had reached such a low point of despair that he had rather die than continue living with the shame of his actions. He just wanted it to be over.

So, he slowly trudged along this dusty road toward the fate of death by stoning at the hands of his father. But then his weary eyes saw something that stopped him cold in his tracks, frozen with fear. He saw the figure of a man walking rapidly toward him. It was his father, and the moment he had so deeply dreaded was near and only moments away.

His father then started running toward him. The young man was tempted to run in the opposite direction and forever avoid this fatherly encounter.

He thought about fighting his father in continued defiance and prolong his life as much as possible. Every human emotion of fear and apprehension gripped his body and immobilized him on the side of that dusty road.

Now his father was running toward him almost breathlessly, and he couldn't imagine why. Was he filled with that much anger and rage? Then, as his father got closer, the young man saw something he could not believe: His father was weeping and joyously shouting praises of thanksgiving. A broad smile of indescribable joy covered his face rather than a scowl of bitterness.

He ran to his son, threw his arms around him, and repeatedly kissed and hugged him. "I've never stopped hoping you would come home, and I've looked for you every day, not knowing if you were dead or alive. I saw you when you were a long way off, and I started toward you as fast as I could to meet you and welcome you home." Suddenly that lifeless, dusty roadside erupted in shouts of joy, love, and reconciliation.

In that moment, through the power of this parable, Jesus told us that a father's power no longer focuses on a legal right to punish, but rather on his loving desire to redeem and restore what was lost through sinful defiance and rebellion. The writer of First John does not say that "God is law"; rather, he states that "God is love."

I have no way of knowing the condition of your life this Father's Day morning, nor how far away from your heavenly father you have drifted. But, if you find yourself wallowing in a pig pen of disillusionment and despair because of mistakes you have made and the painful consequences of poor choices, do not be afraid to go home to your loving heavenly Father. Right now, get up, stop being afraid of God, and go home to Him. His love and His grace are greater than all your sins! You, too, can experience your Father's amazing love, and this can be the greatest Father's Day you have ever known.

Two Determined Old Men

Last week my cousin asked me if I wanted an old hay rake that had belonged to her father and possibly grandfather. Not being one to turn down an offer for an antique farm implement, I immediately said yes. So, for the last several days, I've been trying to figure out how to haul it and how many people I needed to help me load it.

My brother, Randy, is 79 and I'm 75, and this morning we drove down to examine the rake. Well, to make a long story a bit shorter, we two old idiots decided we could pull the rake out of the briar patch, load it on my truck, and bring it home. Who needs help when two old codgers set their mind to do something?

We got one end jacked up on a board, dropped my tailgate, and backed up against the elevated rake wheel. Okay, now what? Simple. Take a deep breath and pick this thing up another foot or so, slide it forward, and get the wheel on the tailgate. Success.

Take a short break, rest a minute, and keep going. Now to get the rest of it on the truck. We found two boards in a trash pile and laid them in the truck bed with the ends under the rake wheel. This would make it easier to slide the rake in the truck bed. Then I put my truck in reverse and slowly backed up as far as I could, with the rake sliding about half way into the truck. So far, so good.

Then we took another deep breath, grabbed onto the other wheel, and lifted the other end of this heavy rake up and slid it as far as it would go into the truck bed, with about a foot of it and the end wheel hanging out. But the wheel was too close to the ground. Another challenge. More boards from the trash pile. Lift the rake up and put boards on the tailgate under the frame so the rake wheel won't drag on the ground. Success.

But now we realized the tongue hung over the truck side way too far and would knock the windshield out of every car we met. So, here's the solution: take the rope we had and loop it around the tongue of the rake, raise it as high as possible, and anchor it to the other side of the truck. Success again.

So, with one end of this hay rake hanging out the back of the truck, and the rake's tongue sticking up in the air high enough to miss windshields and mailboxes, we headed home...slow and easy with emergency blinkers warning people to get out of the way. We looked like the Clampetts moving to California.

We moved it from Baker Road east of Purvis, but we made it, and I have another old hay rake that will look great with a running rose or yellow jasmine growing in it.

If there's something you want to do, and you don't mind looking goofy doing it, and you don't mind getting dirty and sweaty, you can do it. Age is not the issue: Determination will bring you success.

But I have to admit, I have spent some time in the recliner since getting home.

Gleaning in Boaz's Field

In late April, my brother and I planted a garden that included six rows of Contender green beans. We never imagined the abundant harvest awaiting us. The beans germinated within a very few days with almost a 100 percent germination rate. They grew quickly and became loaded with fresh, tender beans.

The beans have now been picked four times and have yielded roughly sixty buckets of green beans. Each bucket normally converts into eight to ten quarts of canned beans. If you think sixty buckets sounds like a lot, realize that number translates into an astonishing 480 to 500 quarts of beans.

We soon started giving them away. My brother and his wife, their daughter and her family, my cousin, my elderly neighbor, two family friends and their families, and even I have all the beans I need. Oh yes, there's still twenty-four pints I have to deliver to two other individuals. Although there were offers to pay, we refused any money and freely gave them to all. Nearly ten different individuals and families have all the fresh green beans they need in the months ahead as a result of God's blessing.

Is there a good sermon to be found among six rows of green beans? Yes, indeed. In the Old Testament Book of Ruth, there is a wonderful picture of God's grace tucked into the legalistic narrative. The old religious law required land owners to allow people to glean around the edges of their fields during harvest so they could have grain for food (Lev. 19:9-10). But remember that these laws were part of the Jewish religious code and did not apply to others.

Ruth was a Moabite who was allowed to glean grain in Boaz's field. She had no legal right to be there. No aspect of the law put grain in her basket. Her presence there was the work of God.

Without getting into all the details about the Book of Ruth, it is a great truth that all of the blessings that later flowed into Ruth's life were not the rewards of the religious law, but rather the abundant, boundless blessings of divine grace. Ruth had no claim to them; they were a gift from God.

Oh, dear Friends, can you not see that we, too, as Christians, are gleaning in Boaz's field in a symbolic way. It is an early picture of unearned, boundless, and abundant grace. The New Testament clearly tells us that we are not under religious law, but are blessed through God's amazing grace.

Just like Ruth gleaning grain, we have no right and no claim to God's bounty of blessings. All that we are, all that we have, and all that we shall be in the kingdom of heaven for all the ages to come is an amazing gift of grace from God through our faith in Jesus.

Ruth could have never imagined the blessings that awaited her when the harvest began, and neither can we.

Consider the Lilies

A few years ago, during my physical and economic prime, I was blessed with earthly possessions that exceeded my earlier dreams. Then, it all changed. Debilitating heart disease and "friends" who rode my coattail to the poorhouse—and who now seldom bother to say hello—left me looking at life from a different perspective.

Now I live mainly on Social Security and other modest sources of irregular income. I own very little. I have a lifetime lease on this house, but I own no portion of it, and my truck is jointly owned with a relative. Clothes, furniture, pots and pans, a few cats and two dogs are it. The wealth of this world holds little attraction to me. It proved to be the source of some of the greatest personal pain in my life. The old expression is true: "I've never seen a hearse pulling a U-Haul to the cemetery."

Are there days when I have moments of worry about the future? Are there concerns about my heart, especially when I have moments of sudden weakness and nearly fainting? Sure, I'm just a fragile old clay pot, as the Bible says, and it comes with the experience of aging. What if something happens to me? How long will I lie here before someone finds me? Those kinds of anxiety questions are real.

And then I consider the lilies. Jesus used the beauty of a flower to drive home one of His greatest lessons about worry and anxiety. When you consider the lilies, you can find the same peace that He described.

These lilies don't obsessively toil and labor for the beauty they possess, and neither are they filled with worry about the future. They simply fulfill each day the purpose that God gave them, and they make life more meaningful for all who see them. To paraphrase Jesus, "Not even Solomon in all his glory, and with all his gold, fulfilled his purpose in life like that."

You may be having one of those stressful Sundays yourself. I understand how you feel. Most people never knew this, but many Sundays left me so physically, emotionally, and spiritually drained that I would get sick. Some of the worst sick headaches I ever endured happened on Sunday.

So can I just say this to you from an old, tired heart full of understanding, compassion, and encouragement: Consider the lilies—everything is going to be okay.

Tempus Fugit

A friend of mine was assisting a lady purchasing a grandfather clock. As with many older and more traditional clocks, the Latin phrase *tempus fugit* (time flies) was beautifully engraved on her favorite clock's ornate faceplate, and, upon seeing that, the lady gushed, "Oh, this is a Tempus Fugit clock. Tempus Fugit has been making clocks a long time!" In some situations, there's just no adequate response.

Honestly, though, some days it really does seem that time flies. On others, it seems to stand still, especially in sickness and turmoil. But time is a fascinating biblical concept and worthy of serious study. The Bible states that God is "from everlasting to everlasting"; Jesus is the "Alpha and the Omega" (the first and last letters of the Greek alphabet) and thus the beginning and the end; the spiritual kingdom which Christians will inherit has been prepared for us "from the creation of the world"; and a gracious gift of our salvation in Christ is "everlasting life."

Eternity is a very long time. Quite frankly, we are unable to comprehend it with our limited understanding. John Newton tried to poetically express it in "Amazing Grace" when he wrote, "When we've been there ten thousand years, bright shining as the sun, we've no less days to sing God's praise than when we'd first begun." As hard as I might try, I simply can't fathom time in that manner.

It leaves me to wonder: Is there such a thing as measurable time and immeasurable time? Yes, but thinking about it taxes your brain a bit. The world's official time keepers rely on an atomic clock for the most precise time measurement that we are capable of performing. A second is the fundamental time measurement that's used, but, brace yourself, a second of time is calculated in a manner that far exceeds what I was taught at Purvis High School.

At its 13th official meeting in 1967, the International Committee of Weights and Measures adopted the following definition: "The second is the duration of 9,192,631,770 periods of the radiation corresponding to the transition between the two hyperfine levels of the ground state of the caesium-133 atom." I'm not exactly sure what that means, but I have a feeling it is more precise than saying a second is about three shakes of a sheep's tail. An atomic clock can theoretically operate for millions of years without losing one second. As mind boggling as that is, consider an even greater truth: The timeless nature of eternal God is beyond that.

Have you ever seriously pondered the immeasurable nature of God, the boundless life of Christ, and the true nature of "everlasting life"? One of the best ways to do that is by studying the divine name "I AM."

And here's what really stretches my thinking ability: When I enter into Jesus' life by covenant faith, I am graciously given the nature of His "I AM" life to be fully experienced in His heavenly kingdom with Him. Thus, my life in Christ will be everlasting, my home in heaven will be eternal, and the blessings I will experience will be measureless.

Time may seem to fly down here, and *tempus fugit* may seem like an accurate description, but there, in the kingdom of heaven, time shall be no more, and you and I, my Christian brothers and sisters, shall be robed in immortality and become timeless and ageless. Ponder that for a moment. Amazing, simply amazing.

April 13, 1948

On this day in 1948 the world's population increased by another screaming little boy. My two older brothers were born at Dr. Polk's office in Purvis, probably because my father couldn't afford gas to get to Hattiesburg, but they decided to splurge with me. He must have sold a hog or an old cow to get the money, and off to the Hattiesburg Infirmary they went.

Mama wanted a girl, because she hated washing dishes and figured she could train me for that odious chore, but my father wanted another field hand to help him chop cotton, and he won out. For all you Purvis folks familiar with the area around Good Hope Baptist Church, there was an old frame house and farm across the road from the church known as "the Colson place," and that's where I was educated in the basic methods of chopping and picking cotton. It's also where I got caught trying to sneak a big stalk of rabbit tobacco back home so I could roll it up in a piece of brown grocery sack and smoke it. As you can tell, I started sinning at a tender age.

If I had been a girl and washed mama's dishes, she was going to name me Pamela. But when I was another boy, she no doubt wanted to name me Delastun, because she probably swore I was the last one, and she may as well give up trying to get kitchen help.

The Good Lord has been amazingly gracious to me during these seventy- five years. I survived the cotton patch, dairy farm, being a high school drop- out for a long while, and setting absentee records at Purvis High School that will never be broken. I was blessed with a good education at Ole Miss and good jobs. I've survived more ailments, heart disease, and vision impairments than I can keep track of.

But for the last fifty years, I've tried to preach and teach the gospel of Jesus Christ as best I can. I have tried to avoid controversy, politics, power, or personal ego. I've just tried to share the truth of the gospel, as I understand it, and let the chips fall where they may. As I've said many times, don't ask me questions nobody can answer. I'm in sales, not administration.

But over these fifty years, I hope I have made a small difference in the world around me. I have done my best to love those who felt unloved, be a friend to the friendless, share the gospel with those never invited to church, encourage the dispirited, and just be a blessing to as many as I could.

Knowing when the sun will set for the last time on the horizon of my life is higher than my pay grade. But when it comes, and it surely will, please know that I'm going to be with the Lord where there's no cotton to pick and no cows to milk. And unlike my present habitation, in the words of the old hymn, it will be a land where I'll never grow old.

A Homelife that Shaped Christianity

The Silent Years

My homelife as a child greatly shaped my adult views about life, and yours probably did, too. But what about Jesus? Have you ever wondered why He had such compassion for the poor, the sick, and why He, more than anyone in His day, sympathized with the plight and struggle of women, especially those who had been coldly, yet legally, divorced by their husband?

Did His mother's courage in facing all that was said about her implant in Jesus the courage and conviction to confront the merciless leaders of a methodical religion, steeped in a thousand years of tradition and ritual, and encourage much needed change that would better reflect God's love and not the laws of man? As He watched His mother's struggle to survive, did Jesus quietly resolve to be as strong and determined as she was?

I've given considerable thought to these questions over the years, and it's my opinion that Jesus' homelife as a child profoundly influenced and shaped His thoughts and actions as an adult much more than we ordinarily think. It is a fascinating study. What you will discover will provide a much deeper understanding of His love and compassion for struggling, ordinary folks like you and me.

Examining scriptural clues of what homelife was like for the young child, Jesus, will be a blessing and an encouragement to you and will deepen your love for and commitment to our Lord.

A Single Mother with a House Full of Kids

I want you to do something unusual before you read further, and don't be shocked. I want you to put aside for a little while your traditional views of Jesus and how He traveled around Israel preaching, teaching, and miraculously healing people. Also, mentally cover all the images of Renaissance paintings you've seen depicting Joseph, Mary, and baby Jesus with a soft, heavenly light glowing around them. It's okay to do this, and it isn't unchristian, irreligious, or sinful. Rather, it's called critical, creative thinking, and it draws you much deeper into God's word.

Instead, I want you to see the childhood homelife of Jesus as it really was, as best I can envision and describe it. I want you to see His life with its everyday struggles, the role of an earthly father who disappeared from Jesus' life at an early age, the struggles of His mother trying to raise several children as an apparent widow, and the loud noise of brothers and sisters fussing, fighting, and clamoring for what food was available, as children are surely inclined to do. The Bible lists James, Joses, Simon, Judas and unnamed sisters as additional children that Mary had after Jesus was born, so there was seldom a quiet moment.

I want you to see Jesus' childhood life as it unfolded each day, and you'll be surprised at how much like your life and my life it was. The wearisome daily struggle for survival; the burden of poverty; the midnight, sleepless crying of a sick child and having very little money or medicine with which to care for them; the daily demands of finding and preparing food, gossiping neighbors, indifferent religious leaders, and the list goes on and on—just like it is for so many of us today.

It was just life. Life with all of its rough edges and raw emotions. Life in a crowded little house with dirt floors, cold, rock walls, and a mud roof reinforced overhead with limbs and sticks.

It was faith alternating with fear, the power of divine promises competing with the frailty of human insecurity and uncertainty, and the bright hope for tomorrow crashing head-on into the dark, painful reality of each day. Just human life as He knew it, and as we know it, and it profoundly shaped Jesus' understanding of God, religion, and His attitude toward all others, even those who caused the most pain in His personal life and in His family's life—those whom He could so easily have hated, but whom He learned to love and pray for. It shaped Him, and this environment and Jesus' reaction to it shaped Christianity and made us spiritually who we are today.

You must realize that when you read the gospel accounts of Jesus' teaching, or hear some powerful sermon about His life and ministry, the divine truths that He spoke were not chiseled in stone like some ancient law that He delivered. Rather, these concepts of our Christian faith formed in Jesus' heart and mind within the confines of everyday life and His observations of the laborious struggle with life and the burdens of religious law, both in His own home and in the lives of ordinary people around Him.

Jesus was a brilliant person, and don't just write that off as Him being filled with divine wisdom as God's Son. He was a keen observer of people and highly perceptive of their attitudes, thoughts, and words that were quietly spoken behind His back, both about Him and His mother. With unusual wisdom, He observed such ordinary things as the cycles of nature and the potential of a grain of seed, and He brilliantly used those as teaching tools.

But these spiritual and intellectual gifts didn't just appear in His adult life. Rather, they were in Him from a tender age and appeared early in His life. The scriptures say that the boy, Jesus, "increased in wisdom and stature, and in favor with both God and man," and there's major truth in that statement. Divine "favor" basically describes something that greatly satisfies God and something with which He is pleased to the highest level. In essence, divine favor describes God's positive reaction to those who only want to do the work that God has called them to do and fulfill His purpose in their life.

Thus, His Heavenly Father was highly pleased in Jesus' early interest and commitment to Him. Others likewise saw a distinct difference in Him as a child and marveled at Jesus' wisdom and maturity.

But it was His statement to His parents when He was twelve years old that revealed the depth of His commitment. While visiting the Temple for religious observances, Jesus became separated from Mary and Joseph. When He was found discussing scripture with the priests, He was scolded for becoming separated, but Jesus responded, "Why did you seek Me? Did you not know that I must be about My Father's business?" The underlying meaning of "business" is a commitment to a specific task or work with diligence, earnestness, and haste.

I am amazed at an underlying truth found here, one that is seldom discussed. Have you ever considered that, under the religious law, Joseph could have had Jesus stoned to death as a rebellious son for making that statement, and Jesus knew that. Here was a twelve-year-old boy, so moved by what He observed around Him, that He was willing to put His life on the line to do something about the injustice He saw and the perversion of God's truth by the religious leaders of His day. That determination never left Him, and it shaped our Christian faith today.

Jesus, Joseph, and the Role of Father

The relationship between Jesus and Joseph is very important, yet somewhat mysterious and unknown. Joseph obviously played a significant role in Jesus' early life by not stoning Mary to death, as he legally could have done because of her pregnancy when they married, and he went to extremes to protect

Jesus from Herod's cruelty by temporarily taking Mary and Jesus to Egypt, but little else is known about their daily relationship.

One would assume that, over time, Joseph described to Jesus all the divine events associated with His birth, including the fact that he was not Jesus' natural father. But others would have assumed that he was, and they would have referred to Jesus as "Jesus, the son of Joseph."

When Jesus was twelve years old, He went with Joseph and Mary to the Temple to observe Passover, and Jesus became separated from them. After a lengthy search, Joseph and Mary found Jesus discussing scriptures with the priests, who were amazed at His understanding and knowledge. When He was mildly scolded for the separation, Jesus responded, "Why did you seek Me? Did you not know that I must be about My Father's business?"

"Business" basically denotes work to which one is fully and earnestly committed without reservation. With this statement, Jesus began His journey to the cross, and "My Father's work" gradually shifted from the carpentry shop to the work God ordained Him to accomplish and finish— our salvation and redemption.

Also, with this statement, Jesus began the transition in His life that provides one of the great foundations of Christianity and one the most meaningful relationships that you and I have with God. With these words, Jesus began a radical redefinition of the ancient role of a father and a transition of our understanding of the motivation of a father in his children's life from a cold, legalistic authoritarian to a merciful, loving redeemer.

In the patriarchal society of that day, a man had total control over his children and grandchildren for as long as he lived. They were his possession, and they derived their personal concept of themselves from him. Even their name often contained a reference to the father through the use of the phrase "son of," such as one of the disciples being called James, the son of Zebedee. The use of "son of" to denote an individual's identity is found throughout the Bible.

The father's influence upon successive generations of descendants was enormous, both for good and evil. When the Bible states that God "visits the iniquity of the fathers on the children to the third and fourth generation," it doesn't mean that God arbitrarily punishes an innocent child for something his grandfather did decades earlier. Rather it means that the divine consequences arising from God's reaction to sin often impact a man's children and grandchildren as much or more than it did the grandfather who caused it. That is still true today.

As He increased in favor with God, Jesus saw God in the role of "father" more than Joseph, and it was from God that Jesus realized that He received His identity, His nature and personality, His purpose in life, and His name. With the statement, "I must be about My Father's work," Jesus began the transition of the term "father" in His own life from "Jesus, the son of Joseph the carpenter," to "Jesus, the Son of God." Interestingly, the Gospels contain no further reference to Joseph after this moment in the Temple. What eventually happened to him is unknown.

However, it was Jesus' use of this phrase that ignited the violent passion of religious authorities, who considered it blasphemy. In fact, one of their main reasons for condemning Jesus was "because He not only broke the Sabbath, but also said that God was His Father, making Himself equal with God."

Jesus not only referred to God as His Father, but He taught and encouraged His followers to do the same, including you and me. You must realize the enormous spiritual challenge they faced in doing so. Religious leaders taught them never to even say God's name out of reverence. Now Jesus taught them to call God, "Father."

In the Sermon on the Mount, Jesus used the phrase "your Heavenly Father," or a similar title, at least sixteen times to describe His listeners' relationship with God. When He concluded, the people were stunned because nothing like this had ever been taught in Israel.

A father had life and death control over his children, and the religious law permitted a father to stone his son to death for disobedience. This distant, demanding, cold authoritarian control was how most perceived the role of a father, and it was how many also viewed God.

But through the parable of the prodigal son, Jesus radically changed the power of a father from the legal demands of religious law to condemn a sinful child to the passionate desire of redeeming love to save that child.

Jesus powerfully changed the concept of "father" from law to love, and that shaped the whole of Christianity and transformed our relationship with God. Just remember that the next time you begin your prayer with "dear heavenly Father."

And all that began when twelve-year-old Jesus determined in His heart that He must "be about His Father's business."

Jesus' Family

The nature and composition of Jesus' actual family is unknown and subject to varying opinions. Many believe that Mary remained a virgin throughout her life (the perpetual virginity of Mary theory), thus enhancing the miraculous, divine nature of Jesus' life.

On the other hand, others believe that the translation of the word "brothers" lends credence to the belief that Mary had several more children after Jesus' birth. As Jesus was teaching in the synagogue, his detractors were astonished at His words and questioned, "Is this not the carpenter, the Son of Mary, and brother of James, Joses, Judas, and Simon? And are not His sisters here with us?" Obviously, Jesus' family was viewed by those who knew Him as including four brothers and an unknown number of sisters. By this time, Joseph is no longer mentioned, and Jesus is referred to as "the Son of Mary."

Depending on the context, the translated word for "brothers" means "from the same womb," and the meaning can also apply to sisters. This argument holds that Joseph had possibly died, and Mary was now the head of her family that consisted of Jesus, His four brothers, and an unknown number of sisters.

Although no direct description of their interaction is given, the relationship between Jesus and His brothers appears to have been somewhat cool. The Gospel of John contains the following example:

> "After these things Jesus walked in Galilee; for He did not want to walk in Judea, because the Jews sought to kill Him. Now the Jews' Feast of Tabernacles was at hand. His brothers therefore said to Him, 'Depart from here and go into Judea, that Your disciples also may see the works that You are doing. For no one does anything in secret while he himself seeks to be known openly.
>
> If You do these things, show Yourself to the world.' For even His brothers did not believe in Him" (John 7:1-5).

Galilee is in the northern part of Israel, and Judea is in the southern part where Jerusalem was located. Because of their disbelief, did His brothers try to force Jesus to go to Jerusalem so that He could get arrested? It's an interesting question.

On another occasion, Jesus was teaching and His mother and brothers came to Him. When told they were outside, Jesus responded, "Who is My mother and who are My brothers?" And He stretched out His hand toward His disciples and said, "Here are My mother and My brothers! For whoever does the will of My Father in heaven is My brother and sister and mother."

This verse is enormously important to our Christian faith, for through this statement Jesus changed the concept of His family from a physical to a spiritual basis. He was no longer limited to four physical brothers, but instead He had a limitless number of spiritual brothers and sisters— whoever does the will of God in faith.

You must realize that includes you and me. The Bible states that, through His resurrection, Jesus became "the firstborn of many brethren," and He created a new family—the family of God. Hebrews 2:11 states, "For both He who sanctifies and those who are being sanctified are all of one, for which reason He is not ashamed to call them brethren."

It is not James, Joses, Judas, and Simon who are Jesus' brothers, including His sisters, but it is also you and me! By our faith in Him and our commitment to doing God's will in our life, we are Jesus' spiritual brothers and sisters. And because we are His family, we can joyfully sing the words of this hymn:

> "I'm so glad I'm a part of the family of God,
> I've been washed in the fountain, cleansed by His blood!
> Joint heirs with Jesus as we travel this sod,
> For I'm part of the family, The Family of God.—
>
> You will notice we say
> "brother and sister" 'round here,
> It's because we're a family and these are
> so near; When one has a heartache, we all
> share the tears, And rejoice in each victory
> in this family so dear."

All faithful Christians believing in Jesus and doing God's will are Jesus' family. And Christianity became the brotherhood of believers.

Jesus and Religion

The first description of Jesus' interest in the Jewish religion occurred when

He was twelve years old and had been taken to the Temple by Mary and Joseph for Passover observances. He became so deeply engrossed in discussions with the priests, who marveled at His wisdom and understanding, that He neglected returning home, and Mary and Joseph later searched for Him.

It would only seem logical that Mary and Joseph would have described the divine nature of His birth to Jesus, perhaps along with His cousin, Elizabeth (John the Baptist's mother), and Jesus would have had a great interest in the history and meaning of Israel's religious law and covenant. That continued throughout His earthly life as He frequently taught in synagogues and at the Temple.

But Jesus saw the purpose of religion differently from others, and it boiled down to exclusion versus inclusion, which is one of the major differences between the Old and New Testaments. In the beginning of the Old Testament, or the old covenant, God chose Israel to be a "special people" who would serve Him as a "kingdom of priests and a holy nation" (Exod. 19:6) and through whom He would bless other nations. But Israel never saw herself in that role and never described her covenant relationship with God as a "kingdom of priests." That concept is not used again for nearly a thousand years until Peter describes the purpose of the church in this manner, calling Christians "a royal priesthood" (1 Pet. 2:9).

Rather than being a blessing to other nations and revealing God's love and mercy to them through the true spiritual meaning of the Ten Commandments, Israel arrogantly considered herself to be God's special people—and everyone else wasn't. They could not imagine that God loved other people as much as they assumed He loved them, and the idea that God "loved the world" did not exist in their thinking.

This may be surprising for some, but the religious law had been modified over the years to fit the prejudices of men, and it compelled one to "love your neighbor and hate your enemy." The "hate your enemy" part was a man-made addition to the law and not a divine instruction. One's neighbor was essentially someone with similar beliefs and ideas, whereas one's enemy was everyone else. Israel basically hated the rest of the world and thought God blessed that awful attitude.

This produced a system of religious law that condemned just about everybody but themselves; made it unlawful to deal with Gentiles (non-Jews); heaped scorn and hatred on those who were different (Samaritans);

unmercifully treated those who were sick, blind, and maimed as being condemned by God (such as lepers); and produced a religious attitude that coldly cared not one thing about the other nations and people of the world. It was religious arrogance and intolerance in its purest form.

Jesus grew up and spent His formative years observing all of this, and He determined in His heart to do something about it. He was spiritually sickened over the hypocrisy of religious leaders craving the approval of men more than the blessings of God. He pointedly denounced the Pharisees and scribes as "the blind leading the blind," and compared them to a pit of poisonous snakes for their public, prideful posturing in doing alms and saying prayers all to be seen by men without any concern about whether their attitudes and actions were pleasing to God.

In direct contrast to this Jewish exclusion of others under the religious law, Jesus declared a radically different new covenant with God based on faith in Him—and not fanatical obedience to the letter of the law—and a covenant focused on the merciful and loving inclusion of all people anywhere in the world. He forcefully and astonishingly stated His point by declaring that, in fact, God so loved the world that He was willing to send and sacrifice the life of His only begotten Son in order to save the world (John 3:16). He could not have stated a truth more directly opposite to the Jewish religious attitude of exclusion than His statement about God's inclusive love for all people of the world. Nothing of that nature and magnitude had ever been spoken in Israel.

Jesus stated openly that He did not intend to destroy the purpose of the law, but instead He desired to give it the spiritual meaning God originally intended. It all hinged on loving God with all your heart, mind, and soul and your neighbor as yourself. Thus, the arrogant lawyer condescendingly asked, "And who is my neighbor?" He was shocked by Jesus' answer. Neighbor was no longer people around you with mutual beliefs and ideas. Your neighbor, according to Jesus, is now anyone to whom you are personally willing to show God's love, mercy, and grace as a living witness of Jesus' redeeming love. Amazingly, through this loving, inclusive attitude, someone you previously hated as your worst enemy can become your best and dearest neighbor. As an example, read the parable of the Good Samaritan and see who met the definition of neighbor. Here's a clue—"the one who showed mercy."

Thus, Jesus sent His disciples to all nations and people of the world making disciples of them and including them in this new "kingdom of priests," regardless of their race, creed, or color. Jesus turned the cold exclusion of others under religious law upside down and brought every person into the inclusion of God's redeeming love through faith, and this redeeming love includes you and me. This inclusive redeeming love for all people is the heart of Christianity, and it should be the heart of every Christian church and every Christian individual.

And it all started in the heart, mind, and homelife of a young boy named Jesus who determined to do the work that His Father had called Him to do and finally make God's chosen and redeemed covenant people a "kingdom of priests" and a blessing to all other people of the world.

Jesus and James

The Bible lists the brothers of Jesus as James, Joses (Joseph), Simon, and Judas (Jude), plus unnamed sisters. The word for "brothers" can be translated "from the same womb," (and it also applies to sisters), although some denominations hold that Mary remained a virgin throughout her life, and the men were Joseph's sons from a prior marriage or they were Jesus' cousins. I am assuming that "from the same womb" means they were Mary's children born after Jesus.

James is usually listed first, implying that he was the oldest of these brothers. The possible relationship that Jesus had with James is intriguing. At first, none of Jesus' brothers believed in Him according to John 7:5, thus apparently meaning they did not believe the accounts of His divine nature and birth. I'm aware this statement might be difficult for some, but if they did not believe in Him, then they also did not believe Mary and Joseph's statements about Jesus' birth and disregarded them as ingenious fabrications to cover the fact that Mary was pregnant when she married Joseph. Her condition would have violated the religious law and would have required Joseph to stone Mary to death, which he refused to do knowing the truth about Jesus.

Is it possible that James, being the oldest of the brothers, was the most outspoken about His doubts and disbelief? Does that account for Jesus' brothers urging Jesus to leave the safety of Galilee and go down into Judea (where Jerusalem is located), knowing that Jewish authorities would arrest Him? Did James gather his brothers and Mary and go to where Jesus was teaching, apparently concerned that Jesus' statements were a sign of mental illness or demon possession, as Jewish leaders often and vocally stated? Did they, as a family, come to Jesus to take Him home and care for Him? It's interesting speculation, but quite possibly the truth.

If James was the most critical among Jesus' brothers, that would help explain why Jesus appeared to James following His resurrection. 1 Corinthians 15:7 lists a number of people to whom Jesus appeared, and James is specifically identified.

That moment changed James' life, as one might expect. He became an ardent believer in Jesus as God's Son, and afterward became a loyal Christian servant of Jesus and a church bishop. Clement of Rome called James the "bishop of bishops, who rules Jerusalem, the Holy Church of the Hebrews, and all the Churches."

James is historically believed to be the author of the Book of James, and it is through statements in the Book of James that one can get a glimpse of Jesus' homelife. If James grew up in the same home as Jesus, then he, too, saw the struggles of His widowed mother, he heard all the merciless gossip about Jesus and also Mary, and he was also troubled by the insensitivity of religious leaders to their plight as a family.

When one begins to carefully examine James' comments about religion, gossip, healing the sick, and other situations, one can put together a graphic picture of James' homelife—and the homelife of Jesus. It was a homelife that shaped Christianity and changed the world. And we today, as Christians, are the recipients of the divine blessings of that homelife.

Mama's Home

The house next door is empty now,
no window light I see.
The blinds are drawn, the door is locked,
'tis a lonely place to be.

How strange to cast a caring glance
to where she oft would be,
and see no more the one we loved,
she's gone, oh can it be!

The one who, for all of us,
tried to be so strong
has given way to death's last call
and left us here alone.

I can hardly bear to look next door,
for in my heart I moan,
for yesterday and the life we shared
when mama lived at home.

Her warm, sweet smile, in memories etched,
will be a treasure for the young,
and the memory of her loving touch
that somehow could right all wrong.

The holidays and holy days
were oft spent at her side,
hearing tales of life from yesteryear
and watching her fill with pride.

She hugged and talked with every one,
and even wiped a tear from an eye,
and felt the love that only mother's feel
as she fed them a fresh baked pie.

Such memories are now our legacy of love,
and in them our minds will roam,
oh blessed place, how sweet the thoughts,
of when mama lived at home.

Her treasured church is not the same,
there's an empty place we see,
where faithfully she served for many years
with those redeemed at Calvary.

With a humble heart, she taught of Christ's love
and sang of His Amazing Grace,
But, oh, how her cares must have faded away
when at last she saw His face.

Oh, sacred, departed soul,
now through heaven free to roam,
rejoice dear friends for the victory she's won,
for mama has now gone home.

Dear living ones, be not dismayed
and think not that what you see is real.
For mama is not dead, but alive in Christ,
not sick, but finally well.

She's joined the saints in eternal praise
and rejoices around God's throne.
Oh blessed, holy, comforting thought,
our dear mama is now at home.

From a Nobody to a Somebody

A religious nobody can become a spiritual somebody through faith. That may sound like a strange statement, so let me explain.

Israel had several prominent religious leaders, some of whom founded schools of religious thought and practice. There were many respected rabbis and scholarly scribes, and most all were widely known, respected, and admired. There was a saying that one who had such influence and impact on others was a "mover of mountains" because he could often accomplish the impossible through his power and influence. Each of these individuals was a well-known "somebody."

Jesus' disciples were the opposite. Twelve insignificant, unimportant men with no influence, accomplishments, positions, or status. Frankly, just a bunch of "nobodys." But Jesus was about to change that in a way they never dreamed possible.

One day Jesus said to them, "...assuredly, I say to you, if you have faith as a mustard seed, you will say to this mountain, 'move from here to there,' and it will move; and nothing will be impossible for you."

And there it is: The key to being a mountain-mover is not status, stature, power, prestige, wealth, wisdom, or importance, which not many of us have, but rather simple faith in Jesus and the power of the Holy Spirit, which all of us can have.

Jesus told His followers, "But you shall receive power when the Holy Spirit has come upon you; and you shall be witnesses to Me in Jerusalem, and in all Judea and Samaria, and to the end of the earth." In other words, the Holy Spirit can take a nobody—just an average, ordinary person—and make a somebody out of them, including you and me. He can work both in you and through you to do the work of Jesus in places and ways that will be a sign and wonder to others. They will look at your life and hear your testimony with awe and reverence, and they will know that God is using you in a powerful way.

But how much faith is "mustard-seed faith"? It is enough to enable you to express the words of this old hymn as your own testimony:

"I am Thine, O Lord, I have heard Thy voice,
And it told Thy love to me;
But I long to rise in the arms of faith,
And be closer drawn to Thee.

Draw me nearer, nearer, blessed Lord,
To the cross where Thou hast died;
Draw me nearer, nearer, nearer, blessed Lord,
To Thy precious, bleeding side.

Consecrate me now to Thy service, Lord,
By the pow'r of grace divine;
Let my soul look up with a steadfast hope,
And my will be lost in Thine."

When His will becomes your will, and His work becomes your work, and His words become your words, and His life becomes your life, then you cease being a nobody and you become a somebody—somebody who can accomplish the impossible in your life and move mountains through your faith.

Searching for the True Meaning of Christmas

"I Am the Bread of Life"

Christmas is more than just the annual end-of-the-year celebration of the birth of a baby. It is much more than that. If we truly want to experience the deeper meaning of Christmas, then we need to downplay the commercialized version of the holiday and instead search for the deeper spiritual meaning of this pivotal moment in Christian history—the birth of Jesus.

The Gospel of John contains seven "I Am" statements of Jesus that amplify both His nature and His ministry. If we look at those statements closely, we can discover an amazing new understanding of the meaning of Christmas and how His statements transform our life, our relationship to Christ, and our celebration of Jesus' birth and His life.

Jesus said of Himself, "I Am the Bread of life." It truly is one of the most remarkable statements in the Bible. Christianity, in its broader and more philosophical meaning, is premised on a life. Allow the Holy Spirit to open and expand your understanding of this idea for a moment.

The Bible describes God's creation in two realms—physical and spiritual. God inhabits the spiritual domain and man inhabits the physical. The nature of life in these two realms is opposite to each other. The spiritual is eternal, whereas the physical isn't. The heavenly kingdom is a peaceful paradise, but the physical isn't. The spiritual is sinless, but the physical surely isn't. So, is it possible that these two realms could possibly be reconciled to each other in perfect harmony, just as God originally intended them to be? Yes. And that eternal reconciliation of man to God is divinely provided to us through one life.

The Bible states that this life has been in the heart, mind, and redemptive plan of God since the creation of the world. God is both Creator and Redeemer, and the one divine means of God redeeming and restoring all that He created is through this one life. This life would uniquely combine the spiritual nature of God and the physical nature of man in a way never before known. This life would be God in human flesh, and no other person in human history would have those qualities.

The words "I Am" denote the concept of "being," and, in their different tenses, describe that which was, is, and shall be into the future. Thus, knowing that man would inevitably fall from his divine, sinless creation, God provided a means for you and me to be redeemed from our sins and restored to the sinless nature of the spiritual kingdom. Our redemption is not through our good works, our religious ritual, or any other physical means. Our redemption and restoration are guaranteed to us through this life that has been in the redemptive and merciful heart of God since the beginning of time, and it is there now, and always will be. This life that God provides to us in order to save us is as eternal and everlasting as is God!

This life is the bridge between the spiritual and physical realms of life, the seen and the unseen, and the perfect and pure versus the tarnished and tainted. This life is all powerful, in contrast to our weakness; this life is focused on God and not on the world; this life is full of love and compassion contrasted with our self-serving ways; and this life is solely about glorifying God and not gratifying ourselves.

This life is spiritually like the manna that mysteriously fell on the Israelites as they journeyed to the Promised Land. This life is God's ultimate Bread of Life. It is what nurtures us on our journey through life to the eternal blessings awaiting us. This life falls on us each day, according to our needs, and it will never be used up, exhausted, or become stale. This life that has existed in the heart and mind of God since the beginning of time is as fresh and powerful today as it was in the beginning, and it will remain that way through all the ages to come.

Jesus said of Himself, "I Am this life, and my life is the Bread of Life that nurtures and sustains you in the kingdom of heaven. It has always been that way, it is today, and it shall remain unchanged throughout eternity." When you commit your life to Jesus in covenant faith, God gives you this eternal life as a free, unmerited gift. This life becomes your life!

I don't think the Good Lord is overly concerned about what's under your tree on Christmas morning. He is far more concerned with whether you have faithfully committed your life to the life that He has provided to you since the creation of the world. Once you experience the life that always has been with God, is now, and evermore shall be, the meaning of Christmas changes for you.

"I am the Resurrection and the Life"

The Gospel of John contains seven "I am" statements of Jesus that expand our understanding of His life, His ministry, and our own Christian life. Three of these statements relate to Jesus' description of Himself as "the life." As we discussed previously, the phrase "I am" denotes unbroken continuity because that which was now is and evermore shall be.

Jesus said "I am the bread of life," and then He added a further dimension to the divine concept of life when He stated "I am the resurrection and the life." Spiritual Christmas is not about decorated trees, gifts, and holiday cheer. We have created all of that for ourselves. There is a profound difference between the divine meaning of Christmas and the human holiday.

Christmas, in its truest meaning, is about God's gift to us of His life. It is so easy to focus on the birth of the infant, Jesus, and not fully realize that His life is the life of God being revealed to us in human flesh, or as the Gospel of John states, "The Word became flesh and dwelt among us...."

In the reality of our human mortality and frailty, we forget one crucial thing about our existence: Death was never divinely intended to be our final estate, and the grave was never intended to be our final home. We brought that on ourselves. When God created Adam, He made him in His image and breathed into him the breath of life. If his life was the image of God and he had the life of God, then death was not a reality for him—until he ruined that promise through sin and rebellion against God.

The reality of death brought fear and uncertainty into our thoughts about the future—about what happens to us after death. The ancient Jewish concept of death was unclear. There was a belief about a place called Sheol, which was thought to be the abode of the dead, and it was believed to be a dark, mysterious, existence that one descended into at death. Others thought that departed souls went to "Abraham's bosom," wherever that was. The uncertainty became centralized in Jewish religious doctrine, with the Pharisees, the most conservative religious party, believing in an eventual resurrection of the dead, and the Sadducees believing there was no resurrection. For them, death was final, and that was the end of it.

Into this fear and uncertainty stepped Jesus with a promise so bold that many found it unbelievable, and that remains true even today: "I am the resurrection and the life. He who believes in Me, though he may die, he shall live." If we are to more fully understand the meaning of Christmas and the gift of life, then we must consider His statement in its broadest meaning.

The resurrection is not just limited to a future event in which we come back to life after we die. We must realize that the resurrection is the full proof that God's life is neither diminished nor impacted by the human experience of death. Death does not exist in the heavenly realm! It never has and never will. Jesus' resurrection from the tomb is proof of that.

If God is life in its eternal nature, then the resurrection means that God has ordained a life from the beginning of time that transcends our human mortality and simply is not touched by death. This life always has been with God, it is now, and it always shall be…eternal and never ending.

Thus, when Jesus said, "I am the resurrection and the life," He clearly identified Himself as the human manifestation of this divine truth. He has always been the resurrection—the opposite of death—and He is now and always will be. Those who believe in Him may stop breathing and their heart may stop beating, and some doctor may say that they are dead—but they are not. Their life through faith in Jesus is no longer human life; rather, in its truest meaning, it is the resurrection life of Jesus—the eternal life of God that was, is, and evermore will be. Thus, Jesus could assure those who believe in Him that "though he may die, he shall live."

If you are a Christian, you must realize that the meaning of Christmas is that this eternal truth has always existed with God, and it was brought personally to you through the birth of Jesus and your faith in Him. Christmas is God's gift of life to you!

The life of Jesus was, is, and always shall be the life of God, and this life is yours as a free gift of grace this Christmas through your faith in Him.

"I am the way, the truth, and the life"

Christianity has a level of logic that we miss in the harried hustle of the holiday season. Yet when we slow down, stop fretting about toys, tinsel, and decorated trees, and quietly ponder what the birth of Jesus means to each of us spiritually and personally, we discover an amazing, life-transforming truth about the real meaning of Christmas that transforms the meaning of the holiday and fills us with abundant peace and joy.

Give yourself a simple test: Look at your right hand and then your left hand. Imagine that your right hand represents the spiritual, heavenly realm of God and His divine nature. Conversely, your left hand represents the physical, worldly realm of man in which we live. Now, bring your hands together and try making them one. You can't. It's humanly impossible. They are forever separate, despite all that you can do.

Consider for a moment that represents the nature of religion and worship. We can raise our hands to God in exalted worship, but we can't make them one. We can clap our hands together in exuberance, praise and joy, but they are not yet one. We can use our hands for great deeds of religious and charitable deeds, but nothing we do in our own human effort can unite them.

But what if in the beginning of time, even before the foundation of the world was laid, God created a life that would indeed accomplish this impossible feat. This life would combine the nature of God with the character of man and be the one life through which God and man could become one in a holy, covenant relationship. This life would be revealed by God in a miraculous way through a virgin giving birth to this Child, and that would be a clear sign to all the world that this Child was in fact God in human life. This Child would be Emmanuel, "God with us."

This life would then be the final and ultimate manifestation of the true nature of God to man. This life would be divine truth living as a human and revealing the truth of God to mankind as no other life had ever done, because this would be God living as a man and showing them His true nature. It would not be some human trying to act godly; rather, it would be God living perfectly as man is supposed to do if he loves the Lord with all his heart, soul, and mind. This life would then be the truth of God.

This life would also be the surest way to experience the true spiritual nature of God. Doesn't it make sense that if this life is truly God in human form, then a close, personal relationship with that life is the obvious way to God? Of all the paths that you can take trying to find God, wouldn't this life be your quickest route to a loving relationship with God? It would not be some religion or ritual you were following to try to find God; it would just be you and Him—no one else in between—and He would be with you and never leave you. That seems perfectly logical to me.

Allow me to do a short paraphrase of Jesus' statement about Himself: "I am this life, and I have been this life since the beginning of time. I am now, and I evermore will be. I am this eternal life of God. Thus, I am the truth of God, and I am the way to God. I always have been, am now, and forevermore shall be the way, the truth, and the life."

This life is God's eternal bridge to man. It is how He joins His life to your life and my life. This life is the life of God's eternal High Priest, the anointed one who brings God to man and man to God in a holy attitude of worship and service. This life is God's sign and witness to man that this is not just some annual, holiday fairy tale, but is indeed the greatest truth ever revealed to mankind.

But how does this change you personally? When you accept the life of Jesus in faith, He enters into the new covenant with you in which His life becomes your life. You become the eternal life that God ordained from the beginning of time, and you become as timeless as God is. That is why it's called "eternal life," and it is given to you as a free gift. You enter into the life of God's High Priest, and your life becomes a bridge between God and man that others may see. That is why our Christian life is called the "priesthood of the believer." You become His living witness, His emissary, and His ambassador to the world around you.

When you enter into a covenant of faith with Jesus, you enter into the way of God, the truth of God, and the life of God—and Christmas takes on an entirely new meaning for you.

"In Him was life, and the life was the light of men." (John 1:4)

Christmas lights are a joyful feature of the life of the Christmas season. But we long ago lost our deeper understanding about the spiritual meaning of the light of Christmas. If we seriously ponder the meaning of this scripture verse, we can find an entirely new spiritual understanding for our celebration of Christmas.

The Gospel of John lists seven "I am" statements by Jesus. Three of them focus on Jesus being the incarnation of the one life God ordained at the beginning of time through which He would fully reveal Himself to man and redeem them from their sin, or at least those who would believe in this life.

From the beginning, light has been a symbol of the purity and holiness of God, and that is reflected in different ways in the Bible, such as the pillar of fire at night that guided the Israelites in the wilderness or the golden lampstand in the Temple. The greatest and most glorious display of the light of God is the life of Jesus. If you closely read John's statement, you will see the direct connection between the life of Jesus and Him being the light of men. That is to say, His life is the eternal, divine light that fully and completely radiates the truth of God in the darkness of the world.

But how does that change your understanding of Christmas? Jesus said, "I am the light of the world. He who follows Me shall not walk in darkness, but have the light of life" (John 8:12). Think about what He said about you in that statement: If you follow Him, you will not walk in darkness, but you, too, will have the light of life. Do you grasp the enormous meaning of that? By placing your faith in Jesus, you will receive the eternal life of God that has existed from the beginning of time as a free gift of grace, and you will become a divine light to the world around you.

Thus, Jesus told His disciples, and He says the same to you and me, "You are the light of the world. A city that is set on a hill cannot be hidden" (Matt. 5:14). That is an amazing promise to you this Christmas Eve, and it will transform your understanding of the meaning of Christmas. You have been given the life that is the eternal light of God, and your life in Christ can be so radiant that no shadow of darkness can possibly hide it and prevent it from illuminating the life of Jesus for others. You become a beacon of hope, encouragement, love, compassion, and faith for all others around you to see. If this life is in you, then your light cannot be turned off by any scheme of evil that the devil may throw at you.

Think of your life in Christ in this manner: Turn off all the lights in the room except the bright star on top of your Christmas tree. See how it glows and illuminates the room with the light of joy? That is you!

Drive around at night and look at all the bright lights adorning the homes of people. The lights radiate a joyous message of peace and joy, and not even the darkest hour of the cold night diminishes their glow. That is your life in Jesus!

"I have come that they may have life, and that they may have it more abundantly" (John 10:10)

Christmas is God's divine gift of life, and that life is given to us through our faith in Jesus. This life has existed in the heart and mind of God since the beginning of time, and it is the bridge that binds us to God in covenant faith. This eternal life of God became human flesh in the birth of Jesus, and the life of God dwelt among us and we beheld the nature of God.

Jesus often spoke of Himself as being this life, and He said that His specific purpose was to give His "sheep" eternal life and security. "My sheep hear My voice, and I know them, and they follow Me. And I give them eternal life, and they shall never perish, neither shall anyone snatch them out of My hand" (John 10:27-28). If you follow Jesus in faith, then you are a "sheep" of His flock, and His message is spoken to you. In your covenant with Jesus, you have been given His eternal life, and you are as safe and secure in your eternal salvation as the power of God can make you. That should give you abundant peace on this Christmas morning.

But Jesus also said that He had come into this world so that we may have an "abundant" life in Him. This life that He gives to us that has existed in the mind of God since the beginning of time, the life that exists now—and always will exist—is the life that empowers Jesus to proclaim "I am" this life. And it is this boundless, eternal life of God that Jesus gives to you and me.

Have you ever pondered why He described it as an "abundant" life? It does not mean a life of physical abundance as some try to make it. In fact, Jesus specifically said that life does not consist of the abundance of things we possess, but many people find it hard to believe Him.

The meaning of "abundantly" describes spiritual life that exceeds our greatest expectation on every level. It goes past the limits of our imagination and is greater than anything we can envision or imagine. It is a life that defies description because no ability of man can grasp the magnitude of our loving Heavenly Father. This life takes us past every known limit of our human frailty and physical limitations and transports us into the boundless, limitless, sinless, perfection of God's heavenly realm, where we shall dwell forever through this life. Your spiritual life in Jesus has no boundaries, no limits, no restrictions, and no end. That is the life that He came to give to you, and give it you abundantly. Surely, that promise of life fills you with unrestrained joy and praise on this Christmas morning.

The true meaning of Christmas is God's gracious gift of eternal life in Jesus.

Rejoice this Christmas Eve. You have been given the life that is the light of men! Let it shine for all others to see.

Winning the Battle Within: Victory Over Anger

"And whoever compels you to go one mile, go with him two" (Matt. 5:41).

Israel was an occupied territory of the vast Roman Empire during Jesus' earthly life, and conditions were harsh and often brutal. As an insight, when John the Baptist preached repentance, a group of Roman soldiers asked what they should do, and John told them to stop intimidating and falsely accusing people and be content with their wages. Underlying that statement is an atmosphere of rough, humiliating treatment, false accusations of revenge, and discontent with soldiers' pay that led to forcefully taking private property for personal use. It was a breeding ground for seething anger.

Most onerous was the Roman soldiers' ability to compel a Jewish citizen to be a burden-bearer for Rome. The Romans borrowed an old Persian practice that became both an important military concept and a constant source of insult and grief to citizens of occupied territories, including Israel. Roman soldiers could temporarily seize a person, animal, or property and force them into transporting Roman equipment or assisting any Roman in his journey. An example is Roman soldiers compelling Simon, a Cyrenian citizen who was coming in from the country, to carry Jesus' cross.

Any Jewish citizen could be required to carry Roman equipment, supplies, or armament for one mile, at which point the soldier could command another individual to carry the load another mile. One can only imagine the anger, disgust, and hatred people felt, but there was no recourse other than compliance. It is easy to imagine the complaining, cursing, and obscene gesturing that occurred during the one-mile journey.

Every Jewish citizen chafed at this requirement, but Jesus used the hated practice to make one of His most startling statements: If compelled to go one mile, instead of dropping the equipment at the end of the mile, one should voluntarily carry the burden a second mile. Any Roman soldier who had pressed a Jewish citizen into service was accustomed to hearing the complaints and cursing and seeing the scowls of disgust and hatred upon completion of the mile. Imagine how shocked the soldier would have been if the individual voluntarily carried the burden an additional mile without compliant.

Jesus used this despised practice to teach that Christian character is strengthened when you go well beyond what circumstances compel and willfully act in a manner of quiet grace that undeniably testifies to Jesus' presence in your life. Discipleship is the spiritual capacity to convert the most stressful, demeaning, and hurtful circumstances you are forced to endure into an opportunity to glorify Christ and His redeeming love. Roman law may have compelled a Jewish citizen to walk the first mile, but redeeming love for one's oppressor compelled the second mile—and the additional miles that might be walked are unlimited.

Only you know who or what is forcing you to walk the first mile, but only you can choose to walk the second mile. Through the power of the Holy Spirit, you can find the spiritual strength to go the extra mile. When you do, here's the spiritual victory you will experience within yourself:

> • The first mile is walked due to demand; the second mile is walked due to dedication.
> • The first mile is servitude; the second mile is servanthood.
> • The first mile is a burden; the second mile is a blessing.
> • The first mile is walked as a victim; the second mile is walked as a victor.
> • The first mile is walked in silence; the second mile is walked in celebration.
> • The first mile is walked as a foe; the second mile is walked as a friend.
> • The first mile is walked in pain; the second mile is walked in praise.
> • The first mile is walked due to duty; the second mile is walked due to discipleship.
> • The first mile is walked through the power of an individual; the second mile is walked through the power of the Holy Spirit.
> • The first mile is walked in the company of fellow sufferers; the second mile is walked in the company of saints.

Christian discipleship is nurtured and matured by going beyond what is demanded and walking the path of a good and faithful servant to the never-reached destination of completed service to Christ on Earth. There is a profound spiritual difference between the mile demanded by circumstances and the miles traveled through consecration. Throughout His ministry, the thrust of Jesus' teaching about discipleship moved His disciples from law to love, obligation to opportunity, and from the least one must do to the most one can do in service to God. The difference in your attitude between the first mile and the second mile is the essence of your Christian discipleship.

At some point in your life, you will face the demand of the first mile brought on by friends, family, fellow workers, or even foes. Those circumstances can be harsh, hurtful, and burdensome and cause you to feel victimized and angry. But, by rising above the pain and humiliation, the second mile is a triumph of your spirit, a celebration of your sanctification to Christ, and a living testimony that your faith in Jesus enables you to bear the burdens imposed by others in a way that leads them to Christ.

That is the victory of the second mile, and it is your personal victory for Jesus that you win within your heart. May God give you the spiritual strength to walk the second mile.

The Forgiveness of Debt

The Holy Spirit will often tap you on the shoulder with the realization that your thoughts and biblical doctrine aren't exactly the same. The concept of debt forgiveness is one of those teachable moments.

The forgiveness of debt is a hot topic of discussion these days, with many vocal and divergent opinions. However, many of us forget that debt forgiveness is one of the foundation principles of our Christian belief.

At the very beginning, God ordained the concept of the Sabbath. It involved far more than just going to church on Sunday, as many today seem to think. In fact, the Sabbath was a unique system of worship that would have separated Israel from all other nations, both in her worship of God and in her love and mercy for others.

The Sabbath was based on a recurring cycle of seven: Every seventh day was set apart and holy unto God; every seven years the ground was to lie fallow and get renourished; and, most significantly, after seven cycles of seven years, every fifty years a Jubilee Year was to be declared. In that most holy year, those in bondage were to be released, land was to be returned to the original and rightful owners, and all debt was to be cancelled and forgiven.

The Jubilee Year was to be a recurring expression and experience of forgiveness, redemption, and restoration. It was to be the joyous celebration of a new beginning, the joy of starting over free from bondage, and all celebrated being free from debt.

From a spiritual standpoint, Jesus once read the passage about "the acceptable year of the Lord" (the Jubilee Year) to worshippers in Nazareth and said, "Today this scripture is fulfilled in your hearing." These words, and others that He spoke, caused them to laugh at Him, ridicule Him, and physically assault Him for sharing this truth.

When Jesus taught His disciples how to pray, one of the key passages of the Lord's Prayer asks God to "forgive our debts as we forgive our debtors." It's instructive to note that our understanding of the joy and relief of being forgiven of our "debts" to God is directly related to our willingness to forgive what we think others owe to us.

The basis of Jesus' ministry can be found in the spiritual meaning of the Jubilee Year: He redeems our past and gives us a new purpose in life; He restores our soul in sinless perfection before God; and He cancels every sin debt that we have created and gives us the joyous celebration of being debt free in His heavenly kingdom.

However, in all of her history, from the beginning until today, Israel has never declared the Jubilee Year. Many in the Christian church have not declared it either. Why? One can only surmise that it's due to the unwillingness to forgive debt.

And You Thought Church Was Boring

The Cat in the Baptistry

Some may think that the role of a pastor is dignified and reserved, filled with godly thoughts and deeds. Well, in fact the opposite can be true, and I thought you might enjoy a few of my not-so-sanctified moments that occurred over the years. Let's begin with the cat in the baptistry.

The country church had a baptistry behind the choir area that was separated from the sanctuary by a curtain that pulled back to both sides. Normally it was closed with both sides touching in the center.

Early one Sunday, I went to the church to turn on the heating system, and I left the side door slightly open. The neighbor's cat could not resist the temptation of the open door and invited himself inside. So, when I entered the sanctuary area to make sure everything was in place for a wonderful worship service, I met this big cat casually walking down the aisle. I had seen all kinds of people in there, but never had I encountered a big, fluffy cat coming forward—even without a hymn or invitation.

Well, I began trying to catch this Baptist feline, because I could only imagine the uproar it would cause if he ran between somebody's legs or grabbed one of the deacons and made him throw an offering plate up in the air. But, like a lot of sinners, he resisted my invitation to come forward.

After several minutes of earnestly pleading, I opted for Plan B, which involved opening the doors and chasing him out of the church. There was one old stubborn deacon that I'd often had the same thoughts about, but that's another story for another day. By now, Mr. Kitty had decided that he had rather remain inside, so he flat out rejected Plan B, but I didn't, so the chase was on. Round and around we went...up one side and down the other...in between pews and under pews...even throwing copies of the Heavenly Highways Hymnal at him couldn't make him go outside.

Finally, I got him cornered in the choir area, and if I could have hit him with a hymnal, we would definitely have had some special music. But, no, he opted to jump through the baptistry curtains and hide somewhere in the baptistry cubicle.

I had run out of time. People would soon begin arriving, and I had to clean the mess up. Church members would not understand why hymnals were thrown around in the sanctuary and the preacher looked like he had been in a wrestling match with the devil.

So, imagine what was running through my mind as we all gathered in the sanctuary to "worship the Lord on this beautiful Sunday and praise and worship in spirit and truth!" What am I going do if that darn cat jumps through the baptistry curtain right on somebody's neck? We're going to have a repeat of the crazy squirrel revival that Ray Stevens sang about. Should I tell them in advance and warn them, or just let it happen and see how many get saved or rededicate themselves to the Lord? I decided to keep my secret between the cat and me.

Well, he decided to remain in the baptistry, and apparently, he found his way out when the doors were opened again. It could have been my singing that forced him to flee.

I've preached several sermons over the years with different thoughts on my mind, but that is one time I spent the entire sermon thinking about what I was going do if I heard a loud cat screech and some choir member on the back row jumped to his or her feet, ripped off their choir robe, and began screaming "Save me, Jesus! The devil done jumped on my back!"

When Poor Eyesight and Poor Hearing Affect Worship

I was a member of First Baptist in Jackson, and I occasionally served on the Usher Committee, helping people find good seating, especially the elderly or anyone with special needs. A young man who was basically blind began faithfully attending, and he used a guide dog for assistance. I would try to seat him in a place where his dog would not be an issue, but I failed on one occasion.

An elderly lady—one of those old Southern proper ladies—needed a seat, and the only place available was on the other side of the blind guy with the dog. When I got her to the pew, I quietly pointed down and said, "Be careful and don't step on the dog," obviously words that she had never heard in church.

"The WHAT?"

I replied, "The dog, mam, don't step on his dog," again pointing down at the guide dog.

"Well, who in the world turned the dogs loose in the church house? I never..." she snorted. I finally got her seated, but I had to go to the front door and have a good laugh.

On another occasion, this young man was a member of a committee on which I served, and we were meeting at night in a room in the church basement area. When the meeting adjourned, rather than leaving, I stayed behind a bit to make sure he got out of the area okay and had a ride home. Suddenly, someone turned the lights out, and it was pitch-black dark. I couldn't see my hand in front of my face.

I asked my young friend, "Do you have a good sense of humor?" and he said he did.

"Well, they've turned the lights out, and I can't see anything. If you and your dog will get me out of here, I'll take you home." He laughed and agreed. So, he held on to his dog, and I held on to his arm, and up the stairs we went. It was truly a case of the blind leading the blind.

Poor hearing can also impact your worship experience. I served as pastor of a small church in Canton for a few months while in seminary, and one of the older deacons had a severe hearing impairment. He was a wonderful old gentleman, but you had to almost yell at him to get him to clearly understand you. I always thought it was interesting, however, that he said "Amen" during the sermon more often than anyone, whether he clearly understood or not. One Sunday he obviously didn't hear clearly.

The Sunday before Easter, I shared a sermon about the meaning of Jesus' death on Friday, and several times in the sermon I mentioned the importance of what happened at 3:00 p.m. on that Friday afternoon...the time Jesus died on the Cross. As usual, he shouted "Amen!" more than once. When the service ended, I stood at the front door greeting those in attendance, and as the old fellow came by, he stopped and said fairly loudly, "Preacher, tell me one more time what it is that we are going to do at three o'clock this afternoon." I just patted him on the back and lovingly said, "It's okay. You can rest this afternoon. It has been taken care of."

And so, it has. If you are a believer in the Lord Jesus Christ, you can rest today. It's all been taken care of.

When The Sound Man Doesn't Quite Understand Your Instructions

One year Christmas occurred on Sunday, and I wanted to do something different to begin the service, so I hatched up this crazy idea about a crying baby. I worked at Forrest General Hospital then, and a lady I knew there had just given birth to a baby boy. So, I went to great lengths to get a tape recorder and get her to record the sounds of her baby cooing and crying and making the normal newborn baby sounds. She did, and the tape sounded very good and totally realistic.

The plan was for me to step to the pulpit and say, "This was the sound that awakened the world on that first, glorious Christmas morning," and the sound guy was supposed to then run the tape of the baby for maybe ten seconds, and then the choir was to joyously erupt with, "Joy to the world, the Lord is come, let earth receive her King." That was what was supposed to happen—but it didn't. The sound man knew the plan and the choir knew the plan, but it didn't go as planned.

The sanctuary was full, and it was a wonderful worship opportunity. I stepped to the pulpit and dramatically proclaimed, "This was the sound that awakened the world on that first glorious, Christmas morning." The sound system operator had accidentally turned the volume up too loud, and then he stopped the tape after only two or three seconds. Rather than hearing the soft, tender sound of a newborn baby cooing, what came out was an ear-ringing blast of "WAAA," and it stopped. I couldn't believe it.

I looked at the congregation, and they looked startled and puzzled. A young girl sitting beside her mother on the second row looked up at her mom and asked (I could read her lips), "Mama, what was that?" The mother shrugged her shoulders and replied, "I have no idea."

Have you ever heard a choir sing "Joy to the World" as the Call to Worship on Christmas morning while most of them were laughing? Well, I have.

I just pretended that was what was supposed to have happened and kept going, but I noticed the little girl ask her mother a couple more times, "But, mama, what was that?" and mama again replied, "Baby, I have no idea."

I wanted to just stop and say, "Little girl, that was supposed to have been the tender sound of a new born baby instead of the sound of a fat possum getting run over in the church driveway."

So, next time I think about starting a service with a recording of a crying baby, trust me, I'm going to plan B.

When Funerals Don't Go As Planned

An elderly member of the church I was serving as pastor passed away, but the burial location was in Louisiana. So, we had two services for her, one at Purvis and the other where she was to be buried. I rode with the funeral director to Louisiana, and after we got the casket into the church, along with some flowers, I needed to find a restroom.

There was one in the basement area and it was not clearly marked, but I entered anyway. After doing what you do in the restroom, I was in front of the mirror combing my hair, adjusting my tie, and trying to make myself look preacherly when I heard the toilet flush. I looked around and the church pianist was coming out of the stall with a somewhat surprised look on her face. I was in the ladies' restroom. I grabbed my coat and ran out the door like my pants was on fire. Throughout the service, I knew better than to look at her or we would have both busted out laughing, which would not be appropriate conduct at a funeral service.

I was about to conduct a funeral for a church member whose family members didn't exactly love each other. Only minutes before the service was to begin, I noticed one lady was about to explode in anger with her face all red and her eyes glaring. I told the funeral director he had better talk to her, or we were going to have a bad situation. He did, and she calmed down.

I rode with him in the hearse to the cemetery, and I asked what it was all about. She wanted to put a live corsage on her grandmother's dress, and other family members refused. I asked him what he said to her. He told the lady that a live corsage on the dress would invalidate the warranty on the casket, and she couldn't do it. I looked at him quizzically and asked, "When was the last time somebody dug up a casket and brought it in for you to do a warranty inspection on it?" He laughed and said, "I can't recall that it has ever happened, but she didn't know that, and we had a peaceful funeral." Well, sometimes you just gotta do what you gotta do.

A minister friend was told that the family wanted to play the deceased's favorite song as part of his funeral service. So, after sharing the personal information about the individual, he said this was his favorite song, thinking he would hear "Amazing Grace" perhaps. Wrong. From the speakers blasted George Jones "He Stopped Loving Her Today." Well, it was his favorite....

A church member was asked to sing at a funeral. He had his music tape all keyed up and ready to go, but when he was introduced, he accidentally hit "Tuner" instead of "Tape" on his sound device, and the congregation was quite surprised to hear "B-95 Weather...."

Another minister friend was asked to conduct a funeral in place of a pastor who was on vacation. He did not know the lady who was deceased, and he assumed she was a devoted church member, a loyal friend, and a loving mother. In his comments about her, he described all these virtues and spoke about how blessed her family and friends were to know her. The mourners were few in number, and many of them stared at the preacher with a blank look on their face. Following the service, a church member eased up beside the minister and said, "Preacher, you didn't know her, did you? Because she was the exact opposite of everything you said about her." Well, at least she got a nice funeral message.

Be Careful About Those Page Three Sins

You probably realize that I have a whacky sense of humor. Well, here's another preacher story, but this only involves me listening.

When I lived in Jackson years ago, a small radio station that played mostly country and gospel would allow a wide range of preachers to buy time and have a radio ministry. One of my favorites was Sister Barbara. She was very conservative, outspoken, and had a booming voice that would get your attention.

One day I tuned in, and Sister Barbara was already into her sermon. She was preaching hell-fire and brimstone and calling down the wrath of God on every sinner in central Mississippi. By what she said, it was obvious that Sister Barbara had written out a sermon that covered several pages and was reading it on the air, complete with all the drama and evangelistic fervor she could muster.

As she concluded, she yelled out at the top of her voice, "Brothers and sisters, you better hear me, and you better hear me good. I tell you that you cannot go to heaven...I'll yell it at you again...you cannot go to heaven if you do them sins on page three!"

May the Lord forgive me, I know she was doing her best, but I had to chuckle and wish I had been listening when she went over the list of sins on page three. But, on the other hand, she might have blown out my speakers.

The Day the Diving Board Collapsed

What do country kids do on a hot August day for fun? They go swimming in whatever water hole they can find. Around where I lived, Boggy Hollow was popular. But my favorite was a private swimming pool that I shared with fifty Holstein cows. It was a cow pond on our dairy farm about a hundred feet wide in each direction and about five feet deep when full. Surrounded on three sides by a red-clay dam, the cows would not only drink water from the pond but also wade out into the water and cool themselves. The pond was in a pasture beside our house and was close enough that it was a very short run from the front porch to the cool relief of the pond water, if I could make the cows get out of the way.

With cows wading in it and doing what cows do, there were probably about ten trillion bacteria in that water, but that just made my immune system stronger. There was nothing more fun than jumping off the porch, climbing through the barbed wire fence, and running like a scared rabbit to the pond and jumping as far out in the water as I could, especially if I had been picking okra and was stinging all over.

The pond was located only a few feet from the main public road, and that location is important in understanding the confusion that erupted the day the diving board collapsed.

Another country boy, who lived a couple of miles away, had an old gray horse that was so skinny he had to lean him up against a tree on a windy day to keep the poor thing from blowing over. I do believe he bought the horse a sack of feed every Christmas and made it last the whole year. He rode the horse everywhere, even into town to go to football practice.

Anyway, he stopped by my house one steamy hot day, and we decided to go swimming in the pond. Of course, he rode his horse to the pond and then made him swim out to the center. The horse was just tall enough for us to climb on his back and dive off. It was an excellent diving board.

Well, this lasted for several minutes, and then the horse just sat down in the pond, with only his head and neck sticking out of the water. We thought we had about killed him, and we were frantic to keep him from drowning. So, I ran to the barn and got a tractor innertube that I sometimes played on in the pond, and we put that around the horse's head and neck, thinking that would keep him from going under until he stood up.

He apparently enjoyed the support and just continued sitting there cooling and keeping us from using him as a diving board. After several attempts to make him stand, we decided to leave him and go get a wish sandwich for lunch—that's when you got bread and mayonnaise, but you wish you had some meat.

There were no cows around, and we were at the house, so all that was visible to anyone driving past was a wet gray horse's head sticking up through a big, black innertube in the middle of the red-clay cow pond. That's when it became funny.

Several cars and trucks drove past, slammed on the brakes, and stopped. You could see a hand and arm come out the truck window pointing to the horse in the pond with its very own floatie around its neck and then slowly drive away.

Hot summer days could be long and boring back in those days. Very few things happened to give you a good, hearty belly laugh. But that all changed one hot summer day for two farm boys when their diving board collapsed and their remedy caused total confusion on Coal Town Road.

I can only imagine the story that got told back at the feed store when some old guy said, "Y'all ain't gonna believe me, but I swear I just seen a gray horse sittin in a dang cow pond with an innertube around his head." His friend probably said, "Luther, you been in the sun too long. Sit down over here and cool off, and I'll get you an RC and a moon pie."

Life was much simpler back then....

What is Truth?

"And you shall know the truth, and the truth shall make you free" (John 8:32)

The televised Watergate hearings into the political shenanigans of President Richard Nixon occurred nearly fifty years ago, which only reminds me of how rapidly time passes. I was captivated by them, and the folksy mannerisms of Senator Sam Ervin, the committee chairman, gave the proceedings an air of validity and authenticity. I believed what I heard was truth, and so did most everyone else.

Sadly, we have become a different nation in our belief about truth in the last half-century. It's not that politicians have suddenly stopped manipulating facts for personal and political gain, for indeed that seems to be inherent in the scheme of things, and I suppose it will remain so.

In my life, I have watched different presidents of the United States shamelessly lie to the American people to justify wars that killed thousands of American soldiers and changed our role in the world, whether it was Lyndon Johnson and the Gulf of Tonkin Resolution or George Bush and his nonexistent "weapons of mass destruction." Over the years it has become increasingly easy to be a disbelieving American because America has lost her fundamental commitment to truth, and that plague goes to the top levels of leadership in this country.

But, the deceptive use of untruth is not new. As Adolph Hitler rose to power, the Office of Strategic Services (OSS), America's first intelligence agency, drew up the following psychological profile of Hitler and his use of untruth:

> "His primary rules are: never allow the public to cool off; never admit a fault or wrong; never concede that there may be some good in your enemy; never leave room for alternatives; never accept blame; concentrate on one enemy at a time and blame him for everything that goes wrong; people will believe a big lie sooner than a little one; and if you repeat it frequently enough people will sooner or later believe it."

History documents the terrible consequences of the "big lie" strategy, but it has been the favorite tool of despots and charlatans through the years.

It is still a force that we must reckon with today. The greatest crisis we face in America is the assault on truth, and it comes from multiple sources. Politicians lie to us to gain political power, advertisers lie about the quality of products to take our money, media news people misrepresent facts to gain a larger audience and increase their revenue, television evangelists lie to their listeners to get more donations, and even some of your trusted church family members will tell untruths about you for the cheap thrill of gossip.

The potential damage to our nation caused by lies cannot be overstated. Without truth and believability, there are no true moral standards, no respect for law and order, no trust in one another, no faith in economic security, no willingness to be led by those in authority, no interest in religion, and no belief that things will get better. And that is where millions of Americans find themselves today. We have become a nation of cynics, doubters, and disbelievers who no longer rely on the moral compass of truth and whose bearing will easily shift, allowing them to believe virtually anything or nothing at all.

If we are wise, we will recognize that America is under attack, but it is a war unlike any we have fought before. Our enemies will not destroy us militarily nor economically by outside force. Rather, the ultimate battleground is our mind and our perception and defense of truth.

Unlike the days of Watergate, today a large percentage of Americans dismiss the sworn testimony of witnesses before a congressional committee as lies and untruth, we attack the sworn affidavits of FBI agents as lies and a witch hunt, we accept as truth that the highest echelons of law enforcement in this nation are not to be trusted or believed, and we discredit the long and laborious work of prosecutors and grand juries who spend hours, days, and months searching for and establishing facts as discredited puppets and political hacks of some misguided prosecutorial fool. We accept as truth the statements of politicians who have a life-long history of public deception, without questioning their motive or agenda, and we willingly share half-truths and misleading news headlines as if they were gospel truth. We are destroying the most essential fabric of a stable society—truth—with our insatiable appetite for untruth.

By the admission of their own agents, the Russian government launched a strategic campaign of misinformation in America years ago to sow social and political discord and to destabilize the structure of our democratic society. Crazy, untrue stories were freely floated around on social media, and concocted conspiracy theories of every sort attacking the trustworthiness of our most basic institutions were launched, and gullible Americans believed those lies and spread them like a wildfire.

And so today the standard response of most Americans is "I don't believe anything I hear anymore, especially from our government." We are the victims of lies and disbelief, and the critical erosion of truth and public confidence that we see around us today is the result.

What, then, do we accept as truth? Until we find that answer, we will not have political reliability, social order, or economic stability. Truth must become the highest priority in every American's life.

In 1776, America made a determination about political truth through the issuance of a Declaration of Independence that changed the world. As a nation, we declared: "We hold these truths to be self-evident, that all men are created equal, that they are endowed by their Creator with certain unalienable Rights, that among these are Life, Liberty and the pursuit of happiness." We accepted as truth the unheard-of concept that the rights of the individual are greater than the power of the king; that those rights are God-given; that those rights are established by God as a political endowment to all future generations of Americans, and that no power of government can take those rights from us.

We declared as a fundamental tenant of American citizenship that those political concepts are "self-evident truths." They require no further elaboration from a politician; they only require belief and commitment by American citizens. It was through those fundamental truths that we became a free nation. You, as a citizen, must realize that truth set us free, and truth will keep us free.

There is a profound difference between truth and untruth. Truth brings people together in a common bond of citizenship; untruth divides, separates, and causes bitterness that destroys us from within. Truth seeks justice, fairness, and freedom for all; untruth subjugates races, ethnic groups, and individuals who are physically different to second-class citizenship. Truth protects the vulnerable; untruth exploits them for political purposes. Those who seek to lead us who speak truth are worthy of our faith and trust; those who speak untruth should be avoided, shunned, and disregarded as purveyors of danger to America.

My grandmother and my mother used to simply state, "The truth will stand when the world is on fire." I'm not sure which scholarly philosopher originally uttered those words, but if my ancestors lived by that truth, then that's all the validation I need. Indeed, as Jesus said, "You will know the truth, and the truth shall make you free." It is acceptable for us to add today—"and the truth will keep you free."

In response to Jesus' statement that He had come to declare the truth of God, Pontius Pilate looked at Him and cynically asked, "What is truth?" In a shocking example of reality experienced by many Americans today, truth stood before Pilate and looked him in the face, and he refused to believe it. He bought "the big lie" and doomed himself. May we as individuals, and as a nation, not repeat his tragic mistake.

Creator God

In the Beginning

When I ponder the majesty of God's creation, I am drawn to the deeper meaning of the first three words in the Bible, and my understanding of their importance has grown over the years. The Book of Genesis derives its name (the beginning) from these three words. But what does "In the beginning" describe? May I suggest another way of looking at their meaning.

The first five books of the Bible were written by Moses. But, given his challenge of leading the Israelites to the Promised Land, I don't think Moses was focused on the beginning of world history or the mechanics or duration of creation. Could it be that Moses was far more concerned with explaining how God entered into a covenant with Israel and chose them to be His nation of priests who would glorify Him in the world? Does "In the beginning" describe what God did in the beginning of His covenant with Israel and the New Covenant with you and me through our faith in Jesus?

If so, then marvel at this truth: Before God created anything else, He created the heavens. But how and for what overall purpose? What is the importance to you and me of heavenly bodies millions of miles away and millions of years old?

First of all, God amazingly made them out of nothing! He spoke them into existence through the power of His word. The Latin phrase *creatio ex nihilo* describes God's singular power to create something out of nothing. Romans 4:17 describes it as His "ability to call into existence things that do not exist." Look at the heavens and ponder the incredible truth that all those stars and planets were originally created from nothing!

But why would God do that? If "In the beginning" describes the beginning of His desire to enter into a covenant with mankind—and the basis of the Bible is the description of these Old and New Covenants—then He lovingly revealed the limitless nature of His love, grace, and mercy through the limitless nature of the heavens.

Think about this: Throughout the Bible, there is an ongoing relationship between God's unseen spiritual heavenly realm and the physical realm of the world. The majesty of the physical is often used to reveal the nature of the unseen spiritual. The Garden of Eden is an example, but Jesus is the ultimate fulfillment. He was the "fullness of the God-head in bodily form," or as He stated, "If you have seen me, you have seen the Father." In His physical nature, Jesus fully revealed God's spiritual nature.

Thus, when God promised Abraham millions of descendants, including all of us who are justified by faith, He told Abraham to grasp the magnitude of His spiritual promise by gazing at the stars overhead in the night sky. Just as the stars were without number, so too would be Abraham's descendants. You must realize that the stars were already in place for Abraham to see when God made this promise to him. The physical stars were there for the glorious purpose of helping Abraham grasp the magnitude of God's spiritual promise to him.

Is it possible that God is saying to us, "You ask how limitless is my love for you? Look at the stars. When you have finished counting them, then you will have some physical idea of the spiritual magnitude of my covenant love for you!"

And thus the Psalmist wrote, "The heavens declare the glory of God; and the firmament shows His handiwork," and "When I consider Your heavens, the work of Your fingers, the moon and the stars which You have ordained, what is man that You are mindful of him, and the son of man that You visit him?" The writer's understanding of God's spiritual covenant with mankind was heightened by observing the vastness of God's heavenly creation, and it can be that way for you and me, too.

When you gaze at the heavens, just realize that it is a physical way to visualize and imagine the limitless magnitude of God's spiritual nature and His boundless, everlasting love for you, and it has been that way since "the beginning."

Prepared for You from the Beginning of Time

Jesus did not come into existence on the first Christmas morning. His earthly, physical life may have, but the eternal, everlasting life of Jesus has been with the Father since the beginning of time. His handprint is on all of God's creation, and there is a specific purpose stated in scripture for all of His creative work.

The writer of Proverbs equates Jesus' eternal life with "Wisdom" and states, "I have been established from everlasting, from the beginning, before there was ever an earth...When He marked out the foundations of the earth, then I was beside Him as a master craftsman "

The Gospel of John states, "In the beginning was the Word, and the Word was with God, and the Word was God. He was in the beginning with God. All things were made through Him, and without Him nothing was made that was made."

Why did Jesus work since the beginning of time to prepare the vast creation of the heavens? Jesus concludes the Parable of the Sheep and Goats with a statement so startling you will be left reverently worshipping in awe and wonder. To the sheep at His right hand (those who follow Him through faith), He will say, "Come you blessed of My Father, inherit the kingdom prepared for you from the foundation of the world."

Gazing into the physical heavens helps you better grasp the magnitude of the spiritual kingdom of heaven. Trillions of miles in distance and millions of years in the making, and what can be seen is only a grain of sand in dimension compared to all that is there. It is amazing, but not as amazing as what it spiritually represents.

Consider a truth that will leave you speechless. Jesus has been working since the beginning of time to prepare the physical heavens as a way to help you visualize the kingdom of heaven—a home that He has "gone to prepare for you." The physical heavens are there to help you better comprehend how much Jesus loves you and to better comprehend the holiness and magnitude of the kingdom of His Father that He has prepared for you since the foundation of the world. Because you are a joint-heir with Christ to all the blessings of the kingdom of heaven, it is your inheritance as an adopted child of God. All of this was done for you!

The Divine Majesty of the Third Heaven

"I know a man in Christ who fourteen years ago—whether in the body I do not know, or whether out of the body I do not know, God knows—such a one was caught up to the third heaven. And I know such a man—whether in the body or out of the body I do not know, God knows—how he was caught up into Paradise and heard inexpressible words, which it is not lawful for a man to utter" (2 Cor. 12:2-4).

What he saw and heard had been eating at Paul for fourteen years, and he could never get the courage to describe it. If he had fully revealed what he had experienced, he knew that he would be stoned to death. For fourteen years, he struggled with what to do, and these words to the Christian church in Corinth was as far as he dared go.

The ancient concept of heaven was three-tiered. The first level was just overhead, where the wind blew and the birds flew. The second heaven was higher and more mysterious. It was where the moon, sun, and visible stars were. But the third heaven was higher and holier by far. It was the vast unknown reaches of the heavens that was the realm of God and the holy angels.

It was to this awe-inspiring, boundless, holy, majestic heaven that the Apostle Paul was transported. And after fourteen years, he still could not be sure whether it was a physical or spiritual experience—he left that to God's knowledge—but he knew beyond doubt that he saw and experienced the indescribable nature of God's heavenly kingdom.

There was a problem, however, with which he had struggled all these past years, and he really didn't know how to put it into words. The Jewish religion was very structured and was bound by rigid, conservative interpretation of scripture and by the traditions of the elders. No variation from these ancient, established beliefs was tolerated. But that wasn't what Paul saw and heard! He saw divine truths about God's love, grace, and mercy—and he apparently heard explanations about God's love (from whom he would not say)—that so vastly contradicted the traditional views of his faith that he simply could not muster the courage to describe what he had experienced. He just said "it is unlawful for me to say what I heard and to tell you what I saw."

It was so much higher, holier, and purer than the ritual of religion here on earth that he would have been called an infidel and killed for sharing it. Despite all his missionary work, his personal sacrifices, and all the letters he wrote that make up a large portion of the New Testament, we still don't know the real truth of what Paul saw and heard. Can you imagine the burden on his heart and soul?

On some clear nights, I look into the sky and I can see the Big Dipper and a few other celestial formations. I arrogantly think I have knowledge about what I see, but I don't. A "light year" is about six trillion miles in distance, and when I try to fathom the heavens millions of light years away, I realize that I can't begin to fathom how vast the heavens truly are. The true nature of the "third heaven" where God abides is beyond my comprehension, and so I marvel in awe and wonder.

We must realize that a physical picture of the heavens can only give us an imaginary vision of the spiritual nature of God's heavenly realm. The physical just helps us to better visualize the spiritual. But as I have gotten older, I am increasingly drawn to thinking about my eternal heavenly home. It's going to be more than I have ever possibly imagined.

And so is God's love, grace, and mercy. I am convinced that His love for all people is greater than many religious traditionalists can accept. I was powerfully called to preach the gospel forty-seven years ago, and I have steadfastly refused to water down the gospel to make it fit the prejudices of men. I have reached out to all races, creeds, and colors of people and invited them to a saving knowledge of Christ and into the fellowship of the church. I have tried to show the same friendship and Christian love to saints and sinners alike. I have shared Jesus' love with people with drug problems, suicidal tendencies, physical and sexual differences, and people who laughed at me and cursed me in return.

But that approach to the gospel has been costly. I've been asked to leave most of the churches I served as pastor; I've been humiliated by denominational leaders to the point of tears; I've been lied about countless times; I've had sand poured in my truck radiator by church members; I've had church members try to destroy me financially and make me lose my home; and the stories I can tell about the gossip are numerous. I am never invited to preach a sermon anywhere, lead a revival, or speak at any event.

Is this self-pity? Not really. It's just my way of telling you that if you dare to share the magnitude of God's love for all people without condition, reservation, or hesitation, you will encounter opposition.

Jesus' love is greater than most people are willing for it to be. It scares them; it rattles their cage in which they have placed all their prejudices; it makes them see themselves for who they really are; and compels them to become the loving person they don't want to be. It is akin to the unstoppable force of the gospel hitting the immovable stubbornness of the human heart at full force.

Christ's love is so boundless, vast, and endless that traditional religious practitioners cannot fathom all it touches. But if God's third heaven can be pictured physically in terms of trillions of miles and billions of years, then the magnitude of His Spirit and of His redeeming love is even greater.

Some may say that it's just too radical to love and befriend those on my Christian "friends list," but if you have ever had a glimpse of the majesty of the third heaven, it surely is hard not to love them in Christ's name and just as hard not to talk about it.

What Shall We Do With This Baby?

King Solomon, a great leader with many attributes, was known for his godly wisdom and wise counsel. Two women brought a baby before him, each claiming to be the mother. They lived in the same house and had both given birth about the same time, but one baby died. The grieving mother took the living baby as her own and substituted the deceased child for the living one. Both women thus claimed the living baby as theirs, and it was left for King Solomon to decide the true mother.

The wise king chose to do something shocking. He ordered that the baby be split down the middle and each woman be given one-half of the child. It was a gruesome proposition that hid the true test of motherhood, but it worked.

The woman falsely claiming the child agreed, but the real mother instead agreed to let the other woman have the child so that it could live. Solomon then knew that the real mother was the one who was willing to sacrifice so that her baby could have life. One woman based her claim on the power of law, but the true mother rested her desire for the child's life in limitless compassion and love. Is there a lesson for us today in this ancient account about motherly love and sacrifice? I think there is.

Political and social forces have brought America to an unprecedented moment in which we are compelled to look afresh at our commitment to human life, especially the life of our most innocent citizens—American babies. These two women are examples of two diametrically opposite forces competing in our nation today. One would demand the right to end a life in order to maintain a legal claim, while the other insists on life, even if she has to let someone else raise the child and provide for its needs. Maybe these two women are the original versions of pro-choice and pro-life.

Personally, I think both of these positions are filled with some degree of hypocrisy and political maneuvering, using innocent babies as pawns. If one advocates the right to choose, then that choice has dire consequences attached. From the moment of conception, one cannot logically argue that this embryo is not a human, because it cannot be classified as "tissue" within its mother, or relegated to any other convenient category that fits a chosen legal argument. It is a human baby, but if one choses to give birth, then the question becomes, "What do we do with this baby?"

Pro-life advocates have never fully answered that question, in my opinion. There is a profound difference between pro-life and pro-birth. Pro-birth screams and demands that all children be given a chance at life, but an equally adamant demand for the long-term quality of that child's life often becomes woefully silent after that.

Mississippi is now at the forefront of the right to life movement, but our state is not at the forefront of providing a quality of life for children born in Mississippi. We close our mouth and sit on our hands when it comes to funding maternal and child care health programs, WIC assistance, increased Medicaid programs to help poor mothers care for their babies, adequate school lunch programs so that impoverished kids can have a good meal, comprehensive early education programs, competitive teachers' pay, and quality school facilities in many areas.

You and I should take this moment in history to ask ourselves a very serious question: What are we going to do with these babies? Unless we become as equally committed to the quality of each child's life as we are to giving them life, then our pro-life advocacy comes up short.

If that is the case, then all we have done is get them born and then wish them well. It is as if we say to these babies, "We got you here, but you are on your own from now on." That is not exactly what is meant by "the wisdom of Solomon."

Lessons Learned by a Frog in a Birdhouse

As I approached my mailbox, I was quite surprised to see a small frog looking at me. There is a little birdhouse attached to the top of the mailbox post for decorative purposes, and the frog had somehow managed to crawl into the birdhouse through the circular opening on the front. I have no idea how it managed to do that, but it did. As I looked at him peering helplessly back at me, I was struck by the reality that his situation mirrored some of the predicaments that we can get ourselves into, often without trying. Weird stuff just happens sometimes.

Have you ever found yourself facing completely unexpected circumstances, or maybe ended up stuck somewhere that you never intended? It's the same feeling that the frog probably had when it looked around and realized that, in some unexplainable way, it had ended up in a bird house. He realized that there's no use trying to explain how he got here, and no one to turn to for help. Instead of happily hopping along on the ground, he's now five feet off the ground with no clue how to get down, without it being painful. To the best of his knowledge, God didn't make any flying frogs, so this is a challenge that he has to face alone.

Trust me, it happens to all of us occasionally in life. If it hasn't, give it time, and you'll probably feel like a frog in a birdhouse one day, too. So, what do you do if that happens? Well, before giving up and just accepting your fate, look for the positives in your situation. This little frog now has a totally different view of life and the world around him. He sees things, and he views others, in a way that he's never experienced before, and that is good. His world view is vastly different than before, and the same can happen to you.

He now has a deeper understanding of how others live, the challenges they face, the daily struggle of birds looking for worms, and he becomes far more understanding of what life is like for others who are different from him. He may even become close friends with the birds who call this home.

The challenge he faces will make him find personal strength and abilities that he's never known before. How he gets down will make him a much stronger and wiser frog. He now has wisdom to share with others that will make life more meaningful for them. It is a wisdom that he can use to inspire other little frogs to be content with who they are and to find the fullness of life where they are. Success isn't always found in trying to climb to the top—it usually is found in facing life one hop at a time.

The same is true for each of us. Be happy with who you are, live life to the fullest where you are, and grow into a wiser and more compassionate person through every circumstance you face in life. Just take today one hop at a time, and you'll make it.

The Joy of Redemption

Sometimes I think we unduly complicate our understanding of God's love for us and we apply descriptive labels to dimensions of His love that take on a life of their own. Redemption is a good example.

The concept of redemption generally describes the cost of your salvation. We think of it as God's willingness to sacrifice the life of Jesus to "buy you back" from the grasp of sin and thereby redeem you, and that is true.

But redemption has a lot to do with your value to God—just as you are. The ancient religious law shunned and condemned sinners, and the scribes and Pharisees judgmentally declared that there was joy in heaven over one sinner who was destroyed.

But Jesus proclaimed the exact opposite. He was a "friend of sinners," and He regularly ate with them and enjoyed their friendship and fellowship. Jesus said there is great joy in heaven, and even the angels rejoice, over one sinner who repents and is redeemed to God.

Why would this be true? Because God places great value on every human life, including yours and mine. That's hard to grasp, but true. Salvation and redemption are not open to just a pious few, but rather to "whoever" will believe. The life of the vilest sinner has enough worth in the eyes of God for Him to give the life of His Son to save that sinner. That is simply an amazing truth about divine love and redemption.

Allow me to give you an example: I often use old pieces of pine and cedar wood in making borders for flower beds in my yard, and some pieces are over one hundred years old. Some might consider them as junk and useless. But that doesn't matter to me. It doesn't matter that they are old, twisted, gnarled, and considered worthless. Rather, I see beauty and value in them, and I place great worth in what they can become in my hands and through my vision for their use. Their past is of no concern; their value lies in what they can become.

Your life is much the same. Some of you feel worthless today; some of you are broken with worry and uncertainty about your future; and some of you are bent with age and your limbs are twisted with disease and disability. You are tempted to feel useless and beyond redemption as if your life is gone and you've been cast aside and left behind.

Oh, do I have some joyous, good news for you! You are exactly what God is looking for. He wants to redeem you from despair and make something of great beauty and worth to Him and others. You're not there yet, the beauty of your redeemed life hasn't fully appeared, and there's still work to do. But you are on the way! When God begins redeeming you, He sees only what He can do with your life, and that is of enormous value to Him. Your worth to God is beyond calculation. You are a person of worth and beauty about to bloom forth in Christ into a life you've never imagined.

The Marvelous Month of Nisan

The vernal equinox, also known as the spring equinox, occurs when the length of days and nights are the same. For most of us, it simply means that spring is officially here and warmer, longer days are ahead.

But if we had lived when Jesus was here on earth, it would have initiated one of the most joyous times of the year. Maybe Easter would have a deeper meaning for us if we could recapture the joy and meaning of the month of Nisan.

The Jewish calendar was based on lunar cycles, or the changes of the moon. The new moon after the spring equinox began the month of Nisan, or "the month of beginning," and it represented the beginning of a new year, new life, a new harvest celebrated through the Feast of First Fruits, the celebration of deliverance through observance of Passover, and the promise of God's blessings.

Think about those for a moment. In this month before Easter, each of us would be spiritually blessed by looking anew at the biblical significance of the ancient month of Nisan and how our Christian life can be enriched by the meaning of the feasts, celebrations, and events that occurred during that month.

Since Nisan celebrates "the beginning," let's begin at the beginning. Do you ever take a moment to reflect back on the beginning of your life as a Christian? Do you recall when you first felt the spiritual stirring in your soul that led you to a lifelong commitment to Jesus as your savior? How much different is your Christian life today than at the beginning? Would you be willing to describe and share your Christian growth with others?

It began for me when I was ten years old. My parents had just divorced, and my mother and my two older brothers and I were trying to operate an impoverished dairy farm. My brothers were fourteen and eighteen years old, still just kids, but all three of us had to work like grown men.

My memory of my beginning moment is still vivid after sixty-five years. We had a little Trutone radio in the dairy barn that was usually drowned out by the sounds of the milking equipment, but we let it blast away. I can't adequately describe the poverty in which I lived, and on this day, I was working barefooted in mud and cow droppings because I had no work shoes. Filthy, fighting flies that were everywhere, upset and unsure about my family, and afraid of the future, I truly felt unloved and alone. But I wasn't.

Suddenly, my attention focused on the voice of a preacher named Billy Graham, who was telling me through that little radio that God knew all about me, about my pain and my fears, and that God loved me so much that He sent His Son to be my savior, if I would just believe and trust Him. For the first time, I spiritually heard the amazing truth of that, and standing there filthy and barefooted in the midst of flies and cow feces, I truly listened to Billy Graham invite me to commit my life to Jesus as my Lord and Savior. It was some period of time later that I publicly professed my faith in Christ, was baptized, and became a member of First Baptist Church in Purvis, Mississippi.

That was the beginning of a life-long walk with God that I never could have dreamed possible as a ten-year-old boy standing in that stinking dairy barn listening to Billy Graham. Never would I have imagined that I would eventually become a Baptist preacher and serve as a pastor for many years. The love of God that Billy Graham told me about was the foundation of preaching the gospel to thousands of people myself, writing two books on the life of Jesus, and sharing hundreds of media devotionals over several years and, God willing, there's more to come.

I hope you can understand that this time of the year is very special to me spiritually. The crucifixion and resurrection of Jesus totally transformed my life, both spiritually and physically. I simply cannot imagine what path I would have otherwise traveled if Billy Graham had not told me about Jesus and His love for me, and I am not embarrassed by the humble nature of my beginning. From that day, it has been a steady climb upward.

What about you? Would you be willing to share the beginning of your walk with Christ with others? Better yet, would you reach out in love to some lonely soul and personally invite them to begin their own journey to Jesus, just as Billy Graham did for me? It will make the marvelous month of Nisan an amazing time of the year for you.

New Life

The ancient Jewish month of Nisan began with the new moon after the spring equinox and ushered in one of the most festive times of the year, such as the Feast of First Fruits and Passover. This "month of beginning" was a rite of spring and celebrated the emergence of new life in crops, flowers, trees, and the birth of livestock and other creatures.

I can understand that, but the meaning of Easter isn't found in brightly colored eggs and little bunny rabbits, so what if we look for the real meaning of new life that this amazing month reveals to us?

The biblical meaning of Easter must be found in one word—life. Think broadly about this for a moment. The Bible describes two realms, heaven and earth, and two forms of life, physical and spiritual. God is spiritual and dwells in His heavenly realm, and physical man lives in the kingdom of the world. It seems like these kingdoms and forms of life are so vastly different and incompatible that they can never be reconciled with one another.

So, does the Bible also describe a way in which these physical and spiritual kingdoms and physical and spiritual life can be bound together in perfect harmony? Yes. Amazingly, this harmonious union can occur only through a covenant of faith and only through one single life—a life that is the perfect life of God and the life of a perfect man. Mankind cannot live in union with God through keeping the requirements of a code of religious law or through the teaching and writings of a prophet, but rather through jointly sharing life made possible through one single life.

The Bible tells us about this life in some fascinating ways. The writer of Proverbs said this life was with God before the foundation of the world was laid. Genesis records that this perfect life was given to Adam in the Garden of Eden so that he could be created in the image and likeness of God, but he destroyed that through sin.

Isaiah, the prophet, said this life would again be miraculously given to man through the birth of a child born to a virgin, and Jeremiah said this life would be the basis of a new covenant between God and man in which God would transform the heart of a man and make a new creature out of him through writing His covenant on man's heart.

John said this life was with God in the beginning and indeed was God. Then, John declared that this life became human flesh and dwelt among us, and we beheld Him, the glory of the only begotten of the Father. This singular life was the light of mankind, but man blindly did not comprehend this truth.

Isaiah also said this life would be the only sacrifice acceptable to God to blot out the sins of man, and thus God's Suffering Servant would singularly bear our sin and inequity so that we might have healing and comfort.

This life allows God's will to be done on earth as it is done in heaven, and thus, through this life, one can live on earth in harmony with God as he would live in heaven. This godly life was fully manifested in the physical human life of Jesus. On Friday before Passover in the month of Nisan, Jesus willingly and lovingly lay down this perfect life, took upon Himself the sinful life of you and me, and was crucified as God's perfect Passover Lamb, thus fulfilling Isaiah's prophesy of the Suffering Servant.

Early on Sunday morning after Passover, this life was again miraculously and explosively magnified in Jesus when He rose from death and triumphantly walked forth from the tomb at the same time the Feast of First Fruits began.

This life then became the divine gift of God given to every person who believed in Jesus as their Lord and Savior, ushering in the harvest of redeemed souls that continues until this day. Since this life existed with God before the world began and will never cease to exist, it truly is the gift of eternal, everlasting life.

When this life is graciously given to you through your faith in Jesus and you enter into the new covenant with Him, you are spiritually reborn in the newness of life, freely forgiven, redeemed, sanctified, and adopted by God as if you were His child, and you are forever sealed into that loving relationship by the power of the Holy Spirit. You are eternally alive in the kingdom of God and in His presence only through this life ordained by God since the beginning of time.

Thus, Jesus said, "I am the way, the truth, and the life. No one comes to the Father except through Me." If you truly want to celebrate Easter, then allow His life to become your life, and in the power and glory of the resurrection, celebrate your new life in Jesus!

The Day the Flying Lounge
Chair Man Disappeared

Several years ago, an inventive and adventurous man from Purvis built a flying lounge chair...well, that's what it looked like. It was an open-seat air frame consisting mainly of an aluminum chair, with wings, and powered by a small gas engine turning a propeller. It actually worked.

One morning he took a flight over the Coal Town Road area where I live, and he unwittingly created more excitement and hysteria than he could have ever imagined. A lady driving down the road spied him flying over an open area and watched him go behind a tree line. She immediately assumed he had crashed, and she called 911 and reported that a strange flying object had crashed in the woods near Coal Town Road.

Within minutes, the Lamar County Rescue units had assembled near Coal Town Cemetery. I think every available unit was there, and they began slowly driving down all the surrounding roads looking for smoke or crash debris. One deputy came to my house and drove over my pastures and into as many wooded areas as he could searching for the crash site. Soon, the air ambulance helicopter arrived to transport any potential victims, and used their waiting time to fly low and slow over the area searching for the crash site.

Finally, someone looked carefully at the description of the strange flying object and put two and two together. Realizing that the woman had described the flying lounge chair guy, someone had the logical idea to call his house and see if he was okay. Indeed, he was...relaxing on his patio enjoying a beverage. The crash of the flying lounge chair had been solved at the cost of a lot of wasted time and hundreds of dollars in unnecessary expenses.

But, in the meantime, wild, unsubstantiated speculation, false theories of what it was and where it crashed, and creative rescue plans ran rampant. Everyone's imagination went home tired and sweaty that morning.

In my childhood days, Dragnet, featuring Detective Joe Friday, was one of my favorite shows. Joe had a standard line in asking questions and searching for truth: "Just the facts."

All the mass confusion of searching for the flying lounge chair man could have been avoided with a few reliable facts up front. The same is true with our political predicament today.

Wouldn't we be better citizens if we stopped spreading all the wild, unsubstantiated stories and causing fear and simply waited for verified facts to emerge? I talked with an elderly lady recently who was in near panic because she thought she was going to lose her Social Security and car because of the rumored plans of a political party. How can we call ourselves Christian when our baseless speculation and rumor mongering is causing such fear and anxiety?

Why don't we all be like the flying lounge chair man: Sit down, be quiet, and wait for the truth to emerge.

Who Ate All My Candy?

Around 1959 our worn-out Farmall Super A tractor backfired for the last time and died. Mama started talking to a salesman named Clyde at McMullan Equipment Company in Hattiesburg about a tractor trade, and we soon had a new International Harvester 240 that was just a slight improvement over the Super A, but at least the front wheels didn't wobble. With a whopping 28 horsepower, it had only six more horsepower than my lawnmower today. But we farmed with that thing for several years.

Well, my mother and father had recently divorced, and tractor trading wasn't all that Clyde and Evelyn talked about. They took a liking to each other and went out to eat a couple of times. One day Clyde brought mama the biggest box of chocolate candy I had ever seen. Clyde didn't know any better, but that was a mistake.

My two older brothers and I were born with a primal craving for chocolate. We made gallons of chocolate milk with the cold dairy milk, and we would even mix just cocoa and sugar and eat that. Almost every time mama would buy groceries from Otis and Ruby Sue Cameron, I would beg her to get me a Holloway All Day Sucker, a chocolate delight so sticky that it would nearly pull the fillings out of your teeth trying to turn loose of it.

That was the only box of candy that my mama had ever received, and she planned to savor the delight over a few days. She gave us boys a few pieces and put the rest in the old curved-glass china cabinet with the crooked front leg.

The next morning, she looked at her box of chocolates and remarked how sweet Clyde was for giving it to her. She left to go to work at Movie Star lingerie plant making ladies' panties—or as Grandma Voss called them "step-ins"—and left Clyde's candy in plain view of three hungry "chocoholic" boys.

When we finished our morning milking chores, it was time for a snack. Our choice was either a cold hog-lard biscuit and a piece of cold greasy bacon left from breakfast...OR Clyde's candy. That box of chocolates sat there inviting us to partake of its pleasure like a perfumed, voluptuous French vixen inviting some love starved soldier boy into the amorous adventures within her private boudoir. A cold biscuit versus Clyde's candy...it was a no-brainer. Years later, a law professor told me about the doctrine of irresistible impulse, but I was already well acquainted with it.

We didn't eat all the candy at one sitting. It took two or three visits to the crooked-leg china cabinet, but by noon all that was left of Clyde's delicious chocolates was an empty box and a pile of wrappers. There's an old expression that you can't unscramble an egg, and you sure can't un-eat a box of candy.

The crime had been committed—or maybe it was a sin to eat mama's candy—and now judgment awaited. I wasn't sure how God would punish gluttony, but I had a pretty good idea what mama's attitude would be. Sure enough, about ten minutes after 4:00 p.m. she came up the driveway and parked in her normal spot under the chinaberry tree in the backyard. I went to the front porch to begin my escape, and I waited and listened through the screen front door. After about three minutes, I heard this loud non-motherly voice of judgment yell, "Who ate all my candy?"

Self-preservation can be a prime motivator for human conduct, and it was for me. Off the south end of the porch I flew, ran past the tung nut trees beside the house, and set a new track record for getting to the dairy barn. I tried my best to hide behind a stack of cow feed Punch Morris had brought until the danger had passed.

But that night I discovered that a mama's love is greater than a devoured box of candy. I knew she was disappointed, but she didn't say much more about it. I was sad about hurting her feelings, and I was glad she didn't get after me with the fly swatter but, dang, Clyde's box of chocolates sure was good.

For supper that night, we had scrambled eggs, a cold hog-lard biscuit, and some greasy bacon. A mama's love can have its limits.

Am I Really Fearfully and Wonderfully Made?

I've thought about life and death a lot recently. I guess you do that a bit more as you get older. But the reality of death, especially untimely death, has become painfully real to me in the past weeks through the deaths of my sister-in-law and a wonderful young Christian man in our community. By all human standards, it was not their time to go, but they did, and both are at home in heaven as I write this. They aren't pondering death any more, but rather celebrating their eternal life given to them through their faith in Jesus.

David, in his poetic writings in the Psalms, made a startling declaration about himself, and our life also, in Psalm 139: "I will praise You, for I am fearfully and wonderfully made." I know God's word is true, but there are some days when I just don't feel like that, and I know most of you have those moments too. Maybe today is one of those times.

But the truth is, despite how we feel or what cares, concerns, and crisis we may face, we are indeed fearfully and wonderfully made. I well realize that discussing biology and human conception in a devotional might seem strange, but this is a truth I have pondered many times. The chances of you being born are beyond calculation. I've read that the odds of winning the big lottery prize is like one in three hundred million. That's about like someone taking a list of every American citizen and making one phone call at random to someone, and your phone rings. Most of us just say that isn't going to happen to me, and we're probably right.

But, (brace yourself for the biology lesson), when you were conceived in your mother's womb, there were well over one hundred million male cells wanting to become you, but only one made it. Look it up if you don't believe me. So, at a minimum, you are a one-in-a-hundred-million miracle. But, hang on, it gets deeper: That same fact is true all the way back to the beginning of time and the beginning of the human race. Every time there was a birth that produced one of your ancestors, that same one-in-a- hundred-million chance occurred with their birth also. So, if you multiply every birth in your ancestry by one hundred million, you get some idea of the likelihood of you being here today. If at any moment of conception in any of those numerous births there had been a different male cell that produced the child, you would not be here.

You have the choice of deciding whether you are merely a product of biological chance, as if you are nothing more than the lucky male cell that won the lottery of life contest, or are you the result of divine providence and godly intent and purpose that goes back to the beginning of time. David declared in an expression of awe and praise, "For you have formed my inward parts; You have covered me in my mother's womb." And for that reason, David, the poetic Psalmist, declared, "I am fearfully and wonderfully made."

"Fearfully" has a unique meaning somewhat different to our current use of the word. It can be used to describe something that is so different and distinct that it must be viewed with reverence because of who made it and how it was made. Your life is not a mere product of random chance, but rather you are a divinely ordained individual whose life and purpose has been in the mind of God since the beginning of time. Your life has purpose and meaning, regardless of the difficult twists and turns that it has taken.

You are also "wonderfully" made. This descriptive word is directly connected to the biblical concept of signs and wonders in which something happens that only could be an act of God, and thus a sign, and it leaves observers in awe and wonder at God's creative ability, and thus it is a wonder. Do you realize what a miracle your life really is?

So, are you "fearfully and wonderfully made"? Indeed, you are! The great tragedy of human life lies in what little value we place on one of God's greatest creations. Human life has little value for many. We hurt and destroy one another, ignore the needs of others, and often curse and condemn God's miraculous creation. We don't take care of ourselves, and we abuse this temple of the Holy Spirit as if it were some seedy warehouse of human woes.

Your life is a divine miracle of God intended to be viewed with respect and reverence for the opportunity God has given you to know and experience life and the blessings of His providence. You are here against all odds. Your life is a divine gift to yourself and others. Live it with reverence, awe, and the sincere desire to glorify God in all that you do.

There will come a time when it will end, and we know not when. That will be it. Your life will never exist again in this human realm for all the ages to come. You should take this living moment of opportunity in God's eternal creation and make a difference, for you have a divine plan and a purpose for your life, and you have been fearfully and wonderfully made!

Are We Really Always on God's Mind?

One of my favorite country songs is Willie Nelson's "Always on My Mind." The lyrics speak of little things that he could have said and done to better express his feelings, but didn't, yet he could croon that, nevertheless, "you were always on my mind." It is indeed a tender expression of love.

King David, the poetic psalmist, expressed similar feelings about his relationship with God when he asked, "What is man that You are mindful of him?" (Psalm 8:4). David was a great man and one of the architects of the nation of Israel. God greatly blessed him, yet he greatly disappointed God on more than one occasion. David could soar to lofty spiritual heights and gloriously proclaim "the Lord is my Shepherd," and he could also sink into the sordid depths of sin where he would plead with God to "create in me a clean heart and renew in me a steadfast spirit." Despite his greatness, he was, after all, just a man struggling with the trials and temptations of human life— not much different from you and me.

There was, however, a thought that seemed to bolster David's faith, and it can do the same for each of us. Despite the uncertainties of each day, David could hardly fathom that God would set His mind and attention on him as much as He did. It was if David asked God, "How and why do You even remember me?" Have you ever had one of those moments when you were tempted to ask God the same question? In moments of the crushing loss of a loved one, or facing the devastating news of a life-threatening diagnosis, or the loneliness of age when it seems that even family and friends have forgotten you because they seldom call or visit, do you ever want to ask God "Have you forgotten me?" I have.

Here is a thought I want you to ponder: It does not matter how dark the midnight hour may be that you are trying to endure; it does not matter how deep in despair you may feel this day; it does not matter how lonely you may be; it does not matter what failure torments your soul; nor does it matter how insignificant you may feel, there will never be a moment when God will have to admit, "I'm sorry, but I forgot all about you." It just won't happen. Why? Because you are always on His mind.

The Battle of Crinum Trench

You're probably thinking this is about some epic military battle that gives greater meaning to the Fourth of July. That would not be correct. It was indeed an epic battle, but it was between man and nature and was fought alongside my driveway between a thirty-foot-long bed of crinum lilies and me.

Years ago, my aunt planted a row of crimson-colored crinum lilies. Over the years, they became matted together through new bulb growth and truly needed to be dug up, separated, and new beds established. It seemed like a nice gardening project to me.

Crinums are part of a large family of lilies that grow from bulbs and produce a long, slender stalk with blooms at the stalk's end. Crinums come in different colors and are a staple of many older Southern flower gardens.

But crinums are like an unwanted houseguest who has worn a hole in his welcome mat. Once you have them, they don't want to leave and will put up a battle to stay where they are. Trust me, I learned that the hard way.

Little did I know the bulbs are huge and grow rather deep. So, when I took my shovel and started to dig them up, I just cut through the bulb because it was so deep. I had to devise another plan, and this required some serious strategic thinking. Then it hit me: Hitch grandpa's old mule-drawn middle buster (a plow that throws dirt to both sides) to the little John Deere tractor and just plow a deep trench and roll those boogers out of the ground like plowing up potatoes. It was a great idea whose time had not come. When the middle buster, with me trying to plow it, hit the end of the crinum bulb bed, the little tractor reared up, dropped back down, and went dead. The point on the plow broke off, and nary a crinum bulb was dislodged.

Well, I'm not one to readily accept defeat, so I had to devise another strategy. I thought about a backhoe or some kind of digging machine. Nope, not happening. I had what I needed before me; I just had to figure out a new plowing procedure.

We got the little tractor fired up again, but this time I plowed up only a few bulbs at a time with my now-snaggle-tooth middle buster, making the plow come out of the ground as soon as it got under two or three bulbs. I basically rooted them out of the ground like a pig digging up buried acorns. This lasted for hours, and there were clumps of crinum bulbs in every direction. I gave away bunches of them and created six new beds in different areas of the yard.

It will take them several years to get as thick as this bed was. But I'm not digging them up again; I'll be in heaven looking down and laughing at the next poor fellow who tries to dislodge them.

By the way, years ago crinums became a favorite flower to plant near a relative's grave because of their beauty and hardiness. Over the years, they earned the nickname of "cemetery lilies," and there are several clumps growing in nearby Coaltown Cemetery.

When I finally won the battle of Crinum Trench, I fully understood how they earned that nickname. Just so you know, when I'm gone, don't plant any around my grave. They're pretty, but they aren't pretty enough for me to be content with those rutabaga-sized bulbs squeezing me out of my final resting place.

Defenders of the Dream

The craggy coastline of Maine first feels the warm rays of God's sun each morning, as if some divine hand of light and warmth slowly begins to awaken a slumbering nation from her sleep. Thus begins another day of the American dream, for the dream is not a nocturnal fantasy, but rather it is a living reality for all Americans—one not dreamed by night but lived by day.

As the Earth's certain rotation brings this great land to the awakening of a new day, the dream begins anew and afresh in the New England fishing villages, spreads to the great cities of the eastern seaboard, and slowly moves across the timeless beauty of the Appalachian and Blue Ridge Mountains. In hamlets, villages, and on farms, the heart of America starts to awaken not from her dream, but rather to her dream.

The melodious calls of the mockingbird and the meadowlark echo through the misty, silent morning of the great Smoky Mountains and through the lofty pines of the southern forests. The mist of the Great Lakes clears way to the freshness of a new dawn as the bustling cities of the Upper Midwest come to life. Slowly, the first light of a new day glistens on the ancient ribbon on water lazily flowing from Minnesota to Mississippi, and breathes life into her dark waters.

The Mississippi, the Ohio, and Missouri, and all their tributaries, silently flow to their great and common destiny in the Gulf of Mexico. All across the vast miles of Texas and Oklahoma, sprawling ranches teaming with cattle showcase the dawn of a new day.

Within moments, this day's dream awakens on the sprawling farms of Minnesota, Wisconsin, Illinois, and Indiana. The verdant corn fields of Iowa and the endless acres of golden wheat in Kansas begin to reflect the warmth and nurture of God's sun. The peaks of the Rockies begin to faintly glow and then break forth in radiance illuminating the streams and valleys of this ageless granite range. The painted deserts of the Southwest in Arizona and New Mexico next awaken, revealing the intricate handiwork of the Great Master.

The ancient forests of redwood, fir, cedar, and spruce of the Northwest begin to softly glow in the sun's warmth, and the cities of the western coastline awaken. The crystal blue water of the Pacific matches the blue morning sky as the great western sea shakes the rocky shoreline of the Pacific coast. And in only a short time, the timeless beauty of Hawaii and the pristine peaks of Alaska welcome the day.

Another day, and America has again awakened to her dream. The American dream is not imagined in the mind, but lived in the heart of her people. From coast to coast and sea to sea, in towns, hamlets, and cities the dream lives. In schools, factories, and on farms, the dream awakens to life. And in home after home, each family and each American awakens to the possibility and pursuit of their on individual dreams.

As America lives this day, she lives the dream of countless millions who can only imagine the reality of freedom, prosperity, and unlimited opportunity for personal expression. Enslaved masses of people across the globe dream of the freedom to determine who shall govern them, what laws they will have, and to freely represent themselves in political thought and action without fear of death or imprisonment. Each day, Americans live this dream.

Each day, millions economically locked in impoverished slums dream of the warmth of home and sufficient food to fill empty stomachs aching with hunger. Each day, Americans live this dream of prosperity. Each day the farmers of Africa and Asia, plowing their oxen, dream of the ability to grow sufficient food to feed their families and nation. Each day, America lives this dream of abundance.

Each day, terrified residents of war-torn countries dream of peace and political stability. Veiled-faced women laboring under the burdens and restraints of ancient male-dominated legal systems dream of escape from second-class citizenship. Each day, that dream is part of American freedom.

Each day, the neglected, underfed, and permanently illiterate orphans of the world dream of learning the truths and mysteries of life. And each day, in countless public and private schools, American children live this dream of knowledge, education, and learning.

Each day, the oppressed minorities of the world, burdened and beaten down by hatred because of the color of their skin, dream of freedom, acceptance, and equal opportunity. And each day, America lives this dream of personal freedom.

Each day, millions throughout the world dream of a life in which they are accepted for who they are, given every opportunity to be all they can be, afforded equal education opportunities, provided the opportunity to pursue whatever profession they choose, allowed to openly and freely worship their God, and live in a comfortable home in a peaceful place. They dream of being accepted and appreciated for the content of their heart, not the color of their skin, the nature of their personal integrity, and rewarded adequately for the toil of their hands. They dream of experiencing life, liberty, and happiness as God-given rights protected by the power of civil law and authority. They yearn for the freedom and opportunity to dream their own dreams and to make their dreams a living reality.

Each day, millions only dream this dream. But each day, millions of Americans live it. Each of us, in our own way, is the embodiment of the American dream. May we as a nation awaken from our slumber to live this dream to its fullness.

As we each reflect on these truths on this Memorial Day weekend, may I take you to an imaginary, hallowed place you might not have fully appreciated, yet one that every American should visit at least once. It is not a physical place constructed of bricks, mortar, and granite. On the contrary, it is a sanctuary of souls built by the blood of those who have given their all to protect and defend this American dream for you and me. Let's simply call this sacred place our Hall of Remembrance.

You can only walk this Hall in total silence and respect, for you will be numbed by what you experience. Lining the walls of this Hall are the portraits of millions of American men and women who have died to defend your American dream. They gaze down into your face and eyes in silence, as if they are wondering what each of us is doing in our own life to preserve, protect, and defend the dream.

Underneath their portrait is not just their name, but a list of their own dreams that died on the field of battle. Silently reflect on all they might have been, all that they could have contributed, and the life they each could have enjoyed, but they sacrificed all of those personal dreams so that you might pursue and live your dreams.

Hear them in your mind softly calling out their last words of love to their mother, their wife, and their children as the darkness of death slowly enfolded them and they drifted into the quiet eons of eternity.

Hear them whispering your name and asking you not to forget them or their sacrifice for you. Never forget they had dreams, too, just as you and I do. What sets them apart is that they sacrificed their dream through uncommon valor so that you and I can live ours. In the annals of American history, there are no greater servants, no greater patriots, and no greater sacrifice for America than that of the men and women enshrined in this Hall of Remembrance.

On this Memorial Day weekend, may each of us express profound gratitude to God for our ability to live the American dream, and may we each thank God for the life and sacrifice of the Defenders of the Dream.

And We Don't Even Know Their Names

Pause for a moment and take a short American History test:

1. How many men signed the Declaration of Independence?

2. Name at least three of them.

3. Whose name is the most prominent on the Declaration?

4. What were the three personal things that each man pledged to support the Declaration?

5. What happened to the men who signed the Declaration of Independence?

How did you do? How many could you answer?

Fifty-six prominent men were brave enough on that hot July day to put everything they had on the line in support of the cause of freedom. Yet most of us can't name any of them, and we have very little knowledge about what their courage ultimately cost them.

John Hancock is the most prominent name. He reportedly stated that he signed his name large enough for King George to be able to read it without using his eye glasses. That's called courage: He may as well have been signing his own death warrant. The prominence of his name became the basis for the expression "put your John Hancock on the dotted line" to signify signing a document.

Each of these men made a personal pledge to support the cause of the Declaration of Independence by a total commitment of their life, their fortune, and their sacred honor. Allow me to phrase that a bit more to the point. Each of these men said, through their pledge, "I will sacrifice my life, I will spend every dollar I have, and I will not compromise my commitment to this cause for freedom, and I give my word of honor to carry out my pledge."

Their pledge cost them dearly. Five signers were captured by the British and brutally tortured as traitors. Nine fought in the Revolutionary War and died from wounds or hardships. Two lost their sons in the war, and two others had sons captured. At least a dozen of the 56 had their homes pillaged and burned. But they remained true to their word, and none of them recanted or retracted their pledge.

Here are their names.

Georgia:
Button Gwinnett
Lyman Hall
George Walton
North Carolina:
William Hooper
Joseph Hewes
John Penn

South Carolina:
Edward Rutledge
Thomas Heyward, Jr.
Thomas Lynch, Jr.
Arthur Middleton
Massachusetts:
John Hancock

Maryland:
Samuel Chase
William Paca
Thomas Stone
Charles Carroll

Virginia:
George Wythe
Richard Henry Lee
Thomas Jefferson
Benjamin Harrison
Thomas Nelson, Jr.
Francis Lightfoot Lee
Carter Braxton

Pennsylvania:
Robert Morris
Benjamin Rush
Benjamin Franklin
John Morton
George Clymer
James Smith
George Taylor
James Wilson
George Ross

Delaware:
Caesar Rodney
George Read
Thomas McKean

New York:
William Floyd
Philip Livingston
Francis Lewis
Lewis Morris

New Jersey:
Richard Stockton
John Witherspoon
Francis Hopkinson
John Hart
Abraham Clark

New Hampshire:
Josiah Bartlett
William Whipple

Massachusetts:
Samuel Adams
John Adams
Robert Treat Paine
Elbridge Gerry

Rhode Island:
Stephen Hopkins
William Ellery

Connecticut:
Roger Sherman
Samuel Huntington
William Williams
Oliver Wolcott

New Hampshire:
Matthew Thornton

As we celebrate this holiday, the least we can do is silently read their names and thank God for their courage, sacrifice, and honor. Without them, there would be no Fourth of July celebration.

A Requiem for Rachel

On a sweltering August evening in 1990, a dear friend suddenly died from an unknown heart defect. She was only twenty-nine. I was asked to have a part in her funeral, and it was a difficult moment for me.

Sometime after that, I began writing a fictional work about a funeral and the different stages of grief that people experience when personal and natural catastrophes unexpectedly happen. The story is unfinished, and in my melancholy moments (which seem to occur more often with age), I pull it and add another page. One day maybe I'll finish it. These are the opening paragraphs:

"It was the summer that everything seemed destined to die. The nurturing rain that normally fell from lofty, white clouds silently floating in from the Gulf of Mexico on gentle southern breezes left in early May, and by August there was a pervasive feeling that life was slowly losing its grip on almost everything. The green summer grass had retreated back into the earth from the blistering heat, leaving only sparse, withered runners tenaciously clinging to the bleached-out earth like reptilian skeletons. The verdant woodlands slowly took on a mellow-brown hue, and the leaves, especially those hanging limply on the dogwood trees, looked as if they had been cut from old parchment paper and temporarily pinned in place.

The blistering sun baked the pale south Mississippi sandy soil from a cloudless, blue-sky day after endless day. Every creature moved slowly and only when necessary. Even the buzzards stopped plying the sky and drifting on the wind because there was no wind.

Mini-cyclone heat devils seemed to gleefully dance across parched, lifeless fields in odd, irregular patterns sending up clouds of dust before disappearing into fence rows overgrown with hedge and honeysuckle, only to dash out and taunt again after regaining their windy strength. The heat was so suffocating that both men and beasts labored to breathe.

It was a joyless time. Smiles were seldom seen and came and went like the skittish appearance of a wispy cloud that dared offer some hope of relief. Time took its toll on hope, and despair reigned in the heat of high noon.

The dreams of a lot of men slowly died that summer. Crops that would feed families and make mortgage payments withered so severely they eventually resigned themselves to nothingness. The tasseled heads of fields of corn that once held such potential now hung helplessly toward the hot earth. Nothing and no one stood tall and straight any more. Everything seemed bowed under the weight of life, as if constantly praying to God for mercy."

That same description seems applicable to this August day in 2023. This is not our first battle with hot, dry weather, and it won't be the last.

Droughts have an interesting place in biblical history. One of my favorites involves the armies of Israel, Judah, and Edom fighting in the hot desert with little water and soldiers dying of thirst. They asked the prophet Elisha for a word from God, and he gave them an instruction that would surely have seemed strange to them, if not ridiculous, given their circumstance. The prophet said, "Thus says the Lord, 'Make this valley full of ditches.'"

Seriously, what would you have done? They were in a pitched battle for survival and dying from thirst, and God told them to start digging ditches to hold all the water that He was about to send to them. And that was indeed the miraculous blessing they received.

Years ago, I read a statement that said, "Don't pray for rain unless you take your umbrella with you!" But sadly, we seldom follow through with that kind of faith.

We are in need of rain, and a lot of it across not just South Mississippi, but also much of the country. It is a critical situation for many people. I want to encourage all of you to pray for a break from this heat and pray for rain divinely sent to water this scorched earth. When you gather in church tomorrow, please have a special prayer for rain.

And when you pray for rain, don't forget to take your umbrella with you— and start digging the ditches to hold the blessings God will send our way.

Finding Faith in a Drought

We do not know her name. We only know she lived near the village of Zarephath and faced dire circumstances as a starving widow with a hungry, malnourished child to feed. The countryside around her village was parched by a prolonged drought that left both people and animals desperate for food and water.

As a widow, she had no one to help her, and she was desperately doing all that she could to keep herself and her child alive. But she had finally exhausted every means of survival she could find, and she became resolved to the fate she knew was upon her. She had only enough flour to make bread one last time, which would surely be followed by a slow, agonizing starvation death.

And then the unthinkable happened. She received a request from a stranger that tested her faith more than anything ever had. A man named Elijah, who was a prophet of God, came into her village asking for food and water.

When she told him she had only enough flour to make bread one last time, the prophet made her a promise so audacious that it was almost laughable. If she would make him bread with her last flour she had for her child and herself, God would providentially bless her so abundantly her supply of oil and flour would never be used up, and she and her starving child would never hunger again. Contrary to all common logic, she believed him, and generations later her oil and flour still have not been used up. They are nourishing you and me through this devotional—consider that for a moment.

Seriously, what would you have done in her situation? Can we really believe that if we entrust every single thing we have—even our last biscuit—to the providence of God, even in the direst circumstances, that somehow and in some way the Lord will make a way for us and supply us with the necessities of life?

Indeed, we can. Psalm 37:25 promises, "I have been young, and now am old; yet I have not seen the righteous forsaken, nor his descendants begging bread."

But we are now in an extreme weather pattern that is causing great concern about the adequacy of food and water for both people and animals. I've known it to be over 100 degrees many times, but I've never seen it this hot for this long. Are there lessons of faith we can learn in a drought? Yes, if we are wise.

We can realize anew how weak and powerless we are over the forces of nature that make our world habitable. We may be able to send a man to the moon and put machines on Mars…but we can't make it rain.

We can spend untold billions of dollars to build hundreds of great universities to educate ourselves and better grasp the meaning of the universe…but we can't make it rain.

We can build complex machines of every description that give proof of our human brilliance…but we can't make it rain.

Polished politicians with their packaged promises, decorated military officers, millionaires with vast wealth, brilliant medical specialists, and esteemed jurists and great legal scholars may attain the height of success in their respective fields…but they can't make it rain.

We have highly educated men and women who devote their lives to studying weather, and they can tell us all about highs and lows and fronts and storms…but not a single one of them can make it rain.

The simplest and most basic necessity of life—a slow, gentle afternoon rain shower—still remains a mystery and a divine blessing from God. We may be smart and innovative about some things, but the things we need most remain beyond our human control. We still can't make it rain.

So maybe the best lesson we can learn in a drought is how weak we truly are—how vulnerable—how totally dependent on God we are. Maybe if we were wise enough to humble ourselves in His presence and offer God every single thing we have—even our last biscuit—then conditions around us would change for the better.

We still won't be able to make it rain, but we will have a much better understanding of the power and holiness of the One from whom all blessings flow.

And those blessings will indeed flow. The drought will end. It will rain again, but only when He is ready to make it rain. And when He is ready, in the words of the old hymn, "mercy drops round us will fall and showers of blessings" will make us rejoice.

If we are faithful and pray, we will soon see this divine weather-truth once again: It always rains at the end of a drought, because that blessing is alone the work of God.

Ten Gallons of Memories

I finally got an old milk can. I've been wanting one a long time because it represents not only family memories, but also a bygone era in Lamar County that will never return.

My first childhood memories, dating back to the early 1950s, involve milk cans just like the one I obtained. My father began operating a small dairy farm when I was just a little boy, barely out of wearing diapers, and milk cans played a pivotal role in our daily life.

Each can held ten gallons of milk and weighed roughly one hundred pounds when full, including the weight of the can. When filled, a tightly fitting lid was secured on the can, and it was then lifted with a rope hoist and placed in the milk cooler. We would usually have four or five cans in the cooler after the evening milking each day. The milk cooler was about six feet square and was full of ice-cold water that chilled the cans of milk. The cooler was insulated, and a pump stirred the cold water around the cans.

But now for the rest of the story—the bad part. A man named Harold Stevens, known as "Foots," drove a milk truck, and he came by every morning about 4:30 and picked up the milk. That meant somebody had to lift those heavy milk cans out of very cold water and place them on an elevated rack so he could get them in his truck. It was a miserable, cold job, especially on winter mornings, and my father hated doing that chore.

There were several other dairies in Lamar County then, maybe as many as fifteen at one time, and Foots picked up milk cans from all of them and hauled the milk to Franklinton, Louisiana every day, seven days a week, where it was processed and bottled. The cans all had a farm number on them—ours was 466—and Foots brought all the empty cans back each morning. He would bring back five cans and pick up five cans, or whatever number we had. He kept up with all those milk cans from each farm and always had it right. He was one hard-working man.

In addition to the dairy, my father also raised cotton, and every year the workers who helped harvest the cotton would put their bottles of "pop" in the cold milk cooler water every morning so they'd have an ice-cold drink at lunch. They were amazed and delighted with the milk cooler.

Later, all these cans were replaced by bulk milk storage and hauling, and the milk cans became relics. But as time went by, the numerous dairy farms gradually went out of business, the herds of dairy cows were sold, including ours in 1967, and the once thriving dairy industry in the area ceased to exist. I'm not aware of any dairy farms in Lamar County today.

Those days are over, but the memories of them are very much alive. When I look at an old milk can, I can still hear Foots Stevens coming down Coaltown Road in the early morning darkness honking his truck horn—if he didn't see any dairy barn lights on—telling my daddy to get the milk cans ready; I can hear J.M. Voss bitterly complaining about having to get wet with ice water at 4:30 a.m. every morning; and I can still see those five milk cans with 466 painted on the side holding one poor farmer's efforts to feed his family by milking a bunch of bony cows twice a day, seven days a week, with no rest or time off.

When my father was hospitalized in 1957, and my parents divorced in 1958, the milk can chore fell on the shoulders of my two older brothers and me. We were aged 18, 14, and 10. Along with my mother, we operated the dairy for the next ten years. Let's just say that we learned how to work at an early age.

So, I'm probably going to paint 466 on my milk can and look at it often. I may occasionally laugh, maybe even cry sometimes, but never forget the abundance of memories this old milk can represents. They are memories, both good and bad, of people, situations, and circumstances that shaped my life. Just one struggling family on a small, impoverished South Mississippi dairy farm working hard and trusting the Good Lord to help us make it. It's where I grew up and got my start in life that has now stretched over seventy-five years. These are my own special memories of "the old home place."

www.ingramcontent.com/pod-product-compliance
Lightning Source LLC
Chambersburg PA
CBHW071318120626
46546CB00002B/364